Climate Change

Debating America's Policy Options

By David G. Victor

A Council Policy Initiative

Sponsored by the Council on Foreign Relations

This volume is the sixth in a series of Council on Foreign Relations Policy Initiatives (CPIs) designed to encourage debate among interested Americans on crucial foreign policy top-ics by presenting the issues and policy choices in terms easily understood by experts and nonexperts alike. The substance of the volume benefited from the comments of several ana-lysts and many reviewers, but responsibility for the final text remains with the author.

Other Council Policy Initiatives:
A New National Security Strategy in an Age of Terrorists, Tyrants, and Weapons of Mass Destruction (2003), Lawrence J. Korb, Project Director; *Reshaping America's Defenses: Four Alternatives* (2002), Lawrence J. Korb, Project Director; *Humanitarian Intervention* (2000), Alton Frye, Project Director; *Future Visions for U.S. Defense Policy* (1998; revised, 2000), John Hillen and Lawrence J. Korb, Project Directors; *Toward an International Criminal Court* (1999), Alton Frye, Project Director; *Future Visions for U.S. Trade Policy* (1998), Bruce Stokes, Project Director.

Council Policy Initiatives are distributed by Brookings Institution Press (1-800-275-1447). For further information about the Council or this book, please write to the Council on For-eign Relations, 58 East 68th Street, New York, NY 10021, or call the Director of Commu-nications at 212-434-9400. Visit our website at www.cfr.org.

CONTENTS

FOREWORD

Climate change is among the most complex problems on the foreign policy agenda. Even with a mounting consensus that humans are causing a change in the world's climate, experts are divided on the severity of the problem and the necessity and nature of policy responses. Practically any course of action implies that today's societies will incur costs as they deviate from the status quo, and any benefits of their efforts will accrue mainly in the distant future. Such intergenerational bargains are always hard to strike.

Compounding the difficulty is the reality that this problem is truly global in scope. A few nations—led by the United States, which is responsible for one-quarter of the effluent that is linked to global warming—account for most emissions. Yet in a global economy some measure of global coordination will be required to ensure that some do not ride free on the efforts of others. This issue thus involves all the factors that make it hard to construct successful foreign policy: highly complex yet uncertain scientific knowledge, widely diverging interests, and the need for effective international arrangements.

In the United States, climate change has become a lightning rod. On one side is a sizable minority that dismisses most or all of the science. There are as well those who view the threats of climate change with such seriousness that nothing less is required than a prompt and complete reorganization of the modern industrial economy—away from the use of fossil fuels (whose combustion emits carbon dioxide, the leading human cause of climate change) and toward some alternative energy future. Bridging this divide will likely prove impossible, and generating a middle position that a credible majority supports will take considerable time. Yet the longer we wait, the more urgent the issue becomes as the concentrations of so-called greenhouse gases build in the atmosphere.

Ever since withdrawing from the Kyoto Protocol in 2001, the United States has incurred widespread criticism for its stance on climate change. But what should guide the federal and state governments as they struggle to craft practical policies on this issue? This is a question more easily asked than answered. As a result, the Council has chosen to tackle this issue by sponsoring a Council Policy Initiative (CPI) rather than seek an unlikely consensus on this highly divisive question.

In this CPI, we present three alternative policy options the United States could pursue. One option calls for modest precaution, including investment in science, voluntary emission reductions, and a rejection of any binding international agreement. A second option seeks to reengage with an improved international agreement—a successor to the Kyoto Protocol—that would set achievable goals for the United States while requiring developing countries to accept binding limits on their emissions. The second option would also create a global system of "emission trading," allowing firms and governments to trade emission credits in an effort to find the most economically efficient solution. A third option would dismiss a global "top-down" scheme and, instead, aim to create markets for new low-emission technologies both in the United States and overseas, notably in developing countries. This last option also envisions the eventual emergence of an international emission trading system, but from the "bottom up" through meaningful national trading systems that could be interconnected over time, much as international currency markets have evolved.

Our goal with this CPI is to present clearly and comprehensively the many issues involved in climate change and the range of options available to policymakers. We aim to draw attention to this important issue and to inform the public on the range of available alternative policy options; we intend to galvanize serious debate rather than to advocate any particular strategy. We use the "three speeches" format because many of the critical federal policy decisions ultimately require the president to give a speech—to articulate the chosen policy and explain why it is superior. We are mindful that this issue cannot be neatly compressed into just three options, and thus a cover memo explains the many dimensions of choice in more detail—from the science to the involvement of developing countries to the role of the president in shaping public opinion.

I thank David Victor for directing and authoring this initiative. He has produced a balanced, comprehensive, and educational book, one that translates the complex and sprawling studies on this issue into simple but sophisticated language. I am also particularly grateful to the advisory committee that helped David strike the right tone while ensuring that the final product reflects a broad range of opinion on this complex issue. Their efforts have produced a timely and thoughtful book.

Richard N. Haass
President
Council on Foreign Relations
June 2004

ACKNOWLEDGMENTS

I am grateful to Richard N. Haass and James M. Lindsay at the Council on Foreign Relations for asking me to direct this study. They tasked Margaret Winterkorn-Meikle at the Council to help with the effort, and for her assistance I am especially thankful. She has learned the essentials of climate science and policy rapidly while managing every aspect of this report with grace and close attention to detail. Her central involvement was crucial to the endeavor.

I have benefited enormously from the stellar and diverse advisory committee members listed at the end of this book. They helped frame the outline for the study and supplied counsel through the writing and editing. We held three off-the-record Council meetings to review a draft—in Washington, DC, with the advisory committee (chaired by Jim Lindsay), as well as sessions with Council members in New York (chaired by Rodney W. Nichols) and in San Francisco (chaired by William K. Reilly). I thank the chairmen and other participants at those meetings for their focused attention and critical comments. In addition, many others helped with detailed written reviews of drafts and with background conversations that have helped me strike the right tone and balance: Paula DiPerna, Paul Epstein, Thomas C. Heller, Fred Krupp, Michael M. May, Martin McBroom, Richard Moss, John O. Niles, Michael Oppenheimer, Glenn Prickett, C. Bruce Tarter, Michael Totten, Christopher Walker, and Robert M. White. At Stanford University, my home base, I am particularly grateful for research and editorial assistance from Becca Elias and Joshua House, and for administrative help from Michelle Klippel. At the Council in New York I thank Patricia Dorff and her colleagues in the Publications Department for ably seeing this through production.

Needless to say, the final book is my responsibility alone. It is customary to say that not everyone who has helped with this study will agree with the conclusions. Often, the author issues that caveat with the secret hope that his powers of persuasion will erase all doubts and every reader will align with his views. In this case, I am certain that nobody will agree with all that I have written, for this book in its entirety is self-contradictory. My aim is to make the best defense for three quite distinct approaches to American policy on climate change. Those three approaches are radically different—supporters of one will be horrified by the others. Where I hope that some common ground will emerge is in the cover memo that unpacks all the major dimensions for policy decisions on this issue. I intend that memo to be a balanced, comprehensive, and digestible treatment of the issues with which a president must grapple.

All I can hope is that the ensuing debate is vigorous and informative. For a decade or so the American people have struggled to find a politically viable strategy to address climate change, and so far we don't have much to show for our efforts. This is an important issue, and we must find a serious approach that is worthy of the stakes.

David G. Victor
June 2004

LIST OF ACRONYMS

°C	degrees centigrade (temperature)
BTU	British thermal units
CAFE	Corporate Average Fuel Economy
CCSP	Climate Change Science Program
CCTP	Climate Change Technology Program
CCX	Chicago Climate Exchange
CDM	Clean Development Mechanism
CEA	Council of Economic Advisers
CO_2	carbon dioxide
DARPA	Defense Advanced Research Projects Agency
DOE	Department of Energy
EMF	Energy Modeling Forum
EPA	Environmental Protection Agency
GATT	General Agreement on Tariffs and Trade
gC/$	grams of carbon emitted per dollar of economic output ("carbon intensity")
GCM	general circulation model
IGCC	Integrated Gasification Combined Cycle
IPCC	Intergovernmental Panel on Climate Change
kWh	kilowatt hours
LNG	liquefied natural gas
mpg	miles per gallon
NAS	National Academy of Sciences
NAST	National Assessment Synthesis Team
NOAA	National Oceanic and Atmospheric Administration
OECD	Organization for Economic Co-operation and Development
PCF	Prototype Carbon Fund
PIPA	Program on International Policy Attitudes
PNGV	Partnership for a New Generation of Vehicles

ppm	parts per million
PUHCA	Public Utilities Holding Company Act
TW	trillion watts (terawatts)
USAID	United States Agency for International Development
USGCRP	United States Global Change Research Program
WTO	World Trade Organization

MEMORANDUM TO THE PRESIDENT

FROM: "The National Security Adviser," "The Director of the National Economic Council," and "The Director of the Office of Science and Technology Policy"

SUBJECT: Policy Strategies to Address Global Climate Change

For fifteen years the U.S. government has struggled with developing appropriate policy responses to the hazards of global climate change. Industrial and agricultural activities, such as burning fossil fuels and clearing forests for crops, cause the emission of carbon dioxide (CO_2) and other "greenhouse gases." As these gases accumulate in the atmosphere, they will trap heat and alter the climate, which in turn will probably raise sea levels and may increase the number and severity of extreme weather events such as heat waves, droughts, and floods. Although often called "global warming," the expected changes in climate are likely to be more complex than a simple rise in global average temperature. For example, possible fluctuations in the Gulf Stream caused by a changing climate could actually cool parts of the North Atlantic region. Climate is naturally variable and humans are highly adaptive, but the effects of climate change could unfold more rapidly than the capacity of humanity and ecosystems to adjust.

Climate change has become a perennial issue on the foreign policy agenda. Because the emissions that cause climate change are global in scope, successive administrations have attempted to coordinate policy with other countries. The United States accounts for about one-quarter of world emissions of greenhouse gases, but our ability to act alone is limited. Industry is wary of potentially costly binding limits on its emissions unless other firms in the global marketplace are required to make comparable efforts.

It has proved particularly difficult to engage developing countries in controlling their emissions. Historically, these countries have accounted for only a small fraction of the greenhouse gases that have accumulated in the atmosphere, but their share is rising rapidly as they industrialize. About half of today's net emissions of greenhouse gases comes from these countries; on a per capita basis, however, emissions from developing countries remain at only one-tenth the level of those from the United States.

In 1992 the United States signed and ratified the United Nations Framework Convention on Climate Change, which established a broad framework for international cooperation on climate change. Today, 187 countries are members of the framework convention—essentially every nation on Earth except Iraq, Somalia, Turkey, and a few others. Widespread membership and compliance reflect the convention's exceedingly modest obligations. For the United States and other industrialized countries, compliance has required developing programs that "aim" to reduce emissions to 1990 levels, submitting reports on emissions of greenhouse gases, and contributing to a special fund that compensates developing countries for the "agreed full costs" of their efforts to comply with the convention's goals. The convention commits all members to work toward the "ultimate objective" of limiting atmospheric concentrations of greenhouse gases to levels that will avoid "dangerous anthropogenic interference with the climate system." This aspirational framework reflected the national interests of the key participants at the time the convention was finalized. Industrialized nations generally sought to control emissions but could not agree on the particular level of effort or on how to share the burden. Developing nations were wary of encumbering commitments and thus agreed only to actions that imposed no cost on their economies.

Most governments, including the Clinton administration, viewed the convention's commitments to control emissions as woefully inadequate. In 1995 numerous governments launched a diplomatic process to strengthen the convention, culminating in the 1997 Kyoto Protocol. Kyoto set targets for the total quantity of greenhouse gases that industrialized countries would be allowed to emit during a specific "budget period" of 2008–2012. (Kyoto is largely silent about obligations beyond 2012.) The protocol would allow countries flexibility in meeting their commitments through a worldwide system of tradable emission credits, modeled on the successful experience with trading air pollution credits in the United States. A utility in the United States, for example, could purchase part of its emission budget from Russia, where limiting emissions is much less costly. Since greenhouse gases mix globally in the atmosphere, this trading system would allow attainment of the environmental objective (less human stress on the climate system) at lower total economic cost.

Kyoto imposed no restrictions on the emissions from developing countries. However, a scheme known as the Clean Development Mechanism (CDM)—largely the brainchild of Brazil and the United States—was intended to encourage foreign investment in projects that yield lower emissions of greenhouse gases. Investors would calculate the level of emissions that would occur with and without their projects; the CDM would award valuable emission credits for the difference. For example, the World Bank has pooled funding from a coalition of twenty-three governments and firms to invest in projects such as a small dam in Chile that produces electricity while avoiding the need to burn fossil fuels and emit CO_2. The investors seek to jump-start the CDM and to get emission credits that they can use back at home; host countries such as Chile welcome the investment.

The Clinton administration never submitted the Kyoto Protocol to the Senate for its consent. When that administration left office, the rules for Kyoto's mechanisms—such as procedures for approving CDM projects and for enforcing compliance—were not yet settled, and thus no government could responsibly evaluate whether Kyoto served its interests. Moreover, Kyoto surely would have been defeated in the Senate. Critics of Kyoto pointed to its lack of binding obligations for China, India, and other developing countries to control their emissions. Imposing Kyoto's emission controls on the United States—a reduction in emissions of greenhouse gases to a level 7 percent below that of 1990—would have been politically and economically arduous. At the close of the 1990s U.S.

emissions were already 15 percent above 1990 levels and rising at 1.3 percent per year. Reversing that trend before 2008 would have been impossible without major economic disruption, and thus any plan for U.S. compliance would have required prodigious use of the international emission-trading system. That implied a large outflow of capital to developing countries (via the CDM) and especially to Russia (via emission trading). In Kyoto, Russian negotiators refused to accept a cap that was more strict than a simple freeze on their emissions at 1990 levels; by the late 1990s, however, the collapse of the Russian economy had closed factories and driven emissions down by nearly 40 percent, and emission projections for 2008–2012 suggested that Russia would have surplus emission credits of roughly one billion tons of CO_2. Selling those credits (mainly to U.S. firms) could have netted Russia perhaps $20 billion to $50 billion, although the surplus would not have been the result of any active Russian effort to control emissions. Critics branded these potential trades as "hot air."

Early in 2001 the Bush administration withdrew the United States from the Kyoto process. It argued that the United States could not meet its Kyoto targets at acceptable cost, and that it was unfair to force U.S. industry to compete in a world economy without meaningful emission controls on all nations.

In February 2002 the Bush administration announced an alternative approach that is based on voluntary actions by firms, investment in research and development on new technologies—such as hydrogen-powered fuel cells for vehicles and advanced low-emission coal plants—and partnerships with key developing countries to assist their application of advanced technologies. President George W. Bush emphasized the large remaining uncertainties in climate science and committed the United States to increasing its investment in scientific research. The technology and science programs committed to in that speech were allocated a total of $4.5 billion in FY03 federal resources, including nearly $1 billion for research on energy efficiency and renewable power. (A copy of that speech can be found in Appendix D.)

While most other nations have remained engaged with the Kyoto process, the Bush administration's dramatic withdrawal from Kyoto galvanized many governments to close ranks and profess their support for Kyoto. Even as public concern about this issue has waned in recent years here in the United States, our allies (especially in Europe) remain deeply concerned and are increasingly frustrated by what they view as an inadequate U.S. response to the problem at hand. Key European nations and Japan, however, are finding that they, too, face difficulty in meeting their Kyoto targets. Many developing countries, which had expected to benefit from new technologies and investments unleashed by the CDM, have grown dissatisfied as a robust market has not yet emerged. The CDM is floundering, in part because it is tied up in red tape and in part because the large potential surplus of emission credits from Russia and other nations that had hoped to sell to the United States has depressed prices and reduced the incentive to invest in projects in developing countries.

With climate change policy in the United States and abroad at a crossroads, you asked us to convene an interagency process to review your options. We find that the issue of climate change is one of the most complex topics on today's policy agenda. It involves most agencies of government, from the federal to the local levels. It requires working closely with Congress and with other nations; if a political deal with one key player unravels, then many others can come unstuck as well. Cutting emissions by more than half over the coming century—a goal that many experts think must be achieved to stabilize human stress on the climate system—implies the need for credible policies that impose costs on society today with uncertain benefits that accrue in the distant future. That intergenerational time scale is longer than most actions of government. Not only is this issue extraordinarily complex, it has also become highly polarizing. At one extreme, climate change is viewed as a hoax or conspiracy dreamed up by scheming scientists who want to usurp government control of the economy and lubricate a gravy train of government research funding. At the other extreme, climate change is seen as a threat so severe that it requires complete and immediate reorganization of the modern industrial economy. The public is deeply confused about the risks and options, offering both the danger that any policy will be easy to parody and the opportunity for you to shape public opinion along the lines most consistent with your favored policies.

Your policy options are not easy to summarize. We have prepared three broad policy strategies, which we present as speeches that you might give in the coming months. All three options recognize that climate change poses varying risks and costs to the U.S. economy and U.S. national security. The speeches differ in their assumptions about the magnitude of climate hazards and in their policy responses.

The first strategy—"adaptation and innovation"—assumes that the hazards from a changing climate are comparable with other environmental challenges that modern society has managed. This strategy advocates expanding current investments in scientific research, improving our capacity to adapt to a changing climate, and devoting resources to new technologies that could allow for lower emissions in the future. This strategy is based, in part, on the assumption that even an aggressive and costly effort by the United States and other industrialized nations would not have much impact on the rapidly rising emissions from developing countries. Climate change is inevitable and thus investments in adaptation are essential. Developing countries have been adamantly opposed to controlling their emissions unless they are fully compensated for the cost. Yet compensation would be extremely costly and adaptation is relatively inexpensive. This strategy also assumes that government resources are best spent catalyzing the development of radical new technologies that can eliminate carbon from the energy system. This speech suggests that special interests have inflated the danger of climate change to serve their needs and warns Americans not to become paralyzed by fear of this problem.

The second strategy—"reinvigorating Kyoto"—follows a radically different approach. It emphasizes that climate change could cause abrupt and potentially catastrophic shifts in weather patterns or sea level. For humans, adaptation could be expensive; for nature, adaptation may be impossible, leading to mass extinctions and the loss of unique ecosystems. With this perspective, the only sensible response is the adoption of aggressive controls on emissions to slow and stop climate change at its root. This speech embraces the process established in Kyoto as the only existing viable international framework. Even as it promises to reengage with that process, it demands reforms that would make Kyoto a much stronger multilateral framework. It advocates aggressive (but achievable) long-term goals for limiting the concentration of greenhouse gases in the atmosphere and mandatory participation of developing countries, with strict penalties for those who do not adhere. It suggests that the need to control carbon is so important that it must become an organizing principle for our foreign and domestic economic policy.

The third approach—"making a market"—also recognizes the need for concerted international action to control emissions. However, it rejects the Kyoto Protocol as an unrealistic, top-heavy scheme. This speech argues that the most effective international regimes, such as the World Trade Organization (WTO), have emerged over many decades from the "bottom up." They are the result of disparate practices that are loosely coordinated through international institutions but rely heavily on strong national institutions and practices. In the case of climate change, this speech emphasizes the need for a diversity of efforts—by key U.S. states, the federal government, other countries, and privately organized systems. It advocates creating emission trading systems in these jurisdictions and then allowing these new "currencies" to establish their value as governments and markets (not international bureaucrats, as in the Kyoto process) determine which systems best combine integrity and efficiency. This speech applauds unilateral action and acknowledges the efforts in some firms and states to begin experimental emission trading. It points to the nascent European emission-trading system as an important experiment, and it suggests that key U.S. jurisdictions explore ways to allow trading between U.S. trading systems and those in Europe. From such productive and experimental exchanges an international market can emerge over time. This speech warns against hasty action to involve all nations in creating this currency, since many—such as Russia and most developing countries—lack both the institutional capacity and desire to control emissions that, together, are essential to ensuring the strength of this new currency.

Each of these three strategies involves lumping together a multitude of detailed policy choices. A real policy could include elements from each. At this pivotal moment we want to ensure that your policy decisions are not constrained by the combinations of choices presented in these three speeches. Thus in this memorandum we unpack the major policy issues in each of six areas where you face choices:

- The scientific assessment of causes and consequences of climate change and policies for supporting additional scientific research;

- Adapting to a changing climate;

- Strategies for controlling emissions;

- Investing in new technology;

- Engaging with key developing countries; and

- Informing the public.

SCIENCE: THE STATE OF KNOWLEDGE AND POLICY CHOICES

In its simplest form, the physical cause of climate change is undisputed. The atmosphere naturally contains greenhouse gases such as water vapor, carbon dioxide, and methane. Absent these gases the planet would cool to a frozen ball, much as the desert chills rapidly on a cloudless night. When humans burn fossil fuels, clear forests, and engage in sundry other activities they pump carbon dioxide and other greenhouse gases into the atmosphere and alter the energy balance of the planet. (Fossil fuels are mainly composed of carbon; burning releases the carbon as carbon dioxide.

Similarly, plant matter and soils contain carbon that is emitted as carbon dioxide through burning or decay.)

The links between emissions of these gases, their buildup in the atmosphere, the ensuing changes in climate, and the ultimate consequences for humans and nature are highly contested. The uncertainties in this long chain—from emissions to consequences—put a premium on policy strategies that adjust easily to changing knowledge.

Climate is naturally variable. Small changes in the Earth's orbit around the sun cause the ice ages and other long-term cycles in climate. Since the depth of the last glaciation—about 20,000 years ago, when much of New England was buried under ice and mammoths roamed in California—the climate has warmed considerably (about 5°C to 7°C, on average). In addition to these orbital gyrations, natural changes in the intensity of the sun also affect climate. Some solar fluctuations occur regularly and are easy to predict, such as the eleven-year cycle during which the sun's output waxes and wanes (it last peaked around 2001). Other changes in the sun have appeared less frequently, yet may have significant consequences. Records of sunspots, for example, suggest that starting around 1645, the sun may have dimmed a total of about 1 percent for seven decades, which coincided with some of the lowest temperatures in the North Atlantic region (and perhaps also globally) during what was already a cold snap—the "Little Ice Age" that began around the thirteenth century and lasted until the nineteenth century. For the most part, such cold temperatures were unwelcome to populations that were already struggling to stay warm and grow crops. Until the very recent concern about global warming surfaced in the 1970s, most studies of climate change focused on natural causes and, interestingly, equated warming with an "improvement" in climate.

Within these natural variations, the fingerprint of human activities is coming into focus. Through burning fossil fuels and deforestation, humans have already caused atmospheric concentrations of CO_2 to rise about one-third, from 275 parts per million (ppm) on the eve of the Industrial Revolution in the late nineteenth century to about 380 ppm today. Global average temperatures have also risen about 0.5°C to 0.9°C during that period, although the warming has not been steady. From 1945 to 1970 the Earth experienced a period of cooling, possibly linked to a slight dimming in the sun and increased output of aerosols (which reflect sunlight back to space) from volcanoes and industrial activity. Since 1970 temperatures have risen; the 1990s were the warmest decade in the industrial era and probably warmer than any other period in the last two millennia.[1] Working with the best computer models of climate—which do a good job of reproducing the historical temperature record—there is a growing scientific consensus that most of the global warming observed in the last fifty years is the result of rising concentrations of greenhouse gases from human-caused emissions. In addition to that observed warming, another 0.5°C of warming is by now "built in" due to the greenhouse gases that have already accumulated in the atmosphere.

As the concentration of CO_2 and other greenhouse gases rises still further in the future, what might be the consequences? The crudest measure of impact is the change in average global temperature from a doubling in the concentration of atmospheric CO_2—a value known as "climate sensitivity." In 1979 the U.S. National Academy of Sciences (NAS) made the first-ever systematic assessment of climate sensitivity and suggested that doubling CO_2 concentration would yield an increase in global temperature of 1.5°C

---

[1] It is difficult to make simple declarative statements about temperature trends because a reliable continuous record of global climate does not exist prior to the late nineteenth century, when global shipping and colonialism allowed the establishment of a global network of somewhat accurate thermometers. To measure earlier climates, scientists must use proxies such as tree rings, ice cores, fossils, ancient Chinese records of sunspots, and other indirect measurements. There are many ways to assemble those proxies into a record of temperature and climate, and some methods yield diverging results. In addition to ground-based measurements since the late nineteenth century, continuous satellite records began in 1979, and there has been considerable controversy over how to square the relatively brief period of satellite measurement with the longer term records from ground-based thermometers, balloons, and rockets. The National Research Council evaluated these issues in 2000, outlined a research program to resolve the outstanding problems, and underscored that satellite and ground-based records alike show that the atmosphere is warming—although each method shows different rates.

to 4.5°C. In recent years more detailed assessments have uncovered many feedbacks that could amplify or dampen the effects of CO_2. Today's best assessments have dramatically increased the range to between 0.8°C and perhaps as much as 8°C, with most studies centered on a value for climate sensitivity of about 2°C.

The most recent full assessment of the science was completed in 2001 by the Intergovernmental Panel on Climate Change (IPCC)—an international assessment process involving thousands of scientists from around the world, including most of the best climate scientists from the United States. The IPCC examined uncertainties in the full chain from emissions of greenhouse gases to changes in climate and concluded that by 2100 the global climate will probably warm from between 1.4°C to 5.8°C. That range is actually wider than that predicted by the previous IPCC study just five years earlier, mainly because the most recent scenarios for emissions of greenhouse gases account for a much greater variety of possible futures and also because new climate models assume a wider range of possible climate sensitivities. In 2001 President Bush asked the NAS to convene a panel of distinguished scientists to review several key questions related to climate change, including the main findings of the IPCC report; the NAS panel reached essentially the same conclusions as the IPCC. (The Executive Summary of that NAS report, which offers a good brief synopsis of major scientific issues, is reproduced in Appendix C.)

We find it striking that more than two decades of intense research, reflecting a total investment of perhaps as much as $30 billion worldwide, has actually expanded the estimated change in temperature. That investment has not narrowed any key estimates of other changes in climate, such as the frequency and intensity of storms or the risks of drought. As scientists have learned more about the climate system, they have uncovered a vast field of unturned stones (see Box 1).

BOX 1

Uncertainties in Climate Science

The list of uncertainties in climate science is long. Five categories of unknowns presently dominate the scientific debate and are especially relevant for policy decisions:

- **Climate Feedbacks.** A wide range of processes affects the sensitivity of climate to changes in the concentration of greenhouse gases. For example, when glaciers and ice sheets melt, the reflectivity of the planet changes—bright ice becomes darker soil and ocean, which absorb more solar energy and thus cause additional warming. Today, clouds probably account for the greatest uncertainties in these feedback effects. Some types of clouds warm the planet; in the last century, for example, a measurable increase in overcast skies is consistent with an observed rise in average nighttime temperatures. Other clouds that are particularly bright and reflective cause cooling. The balance of forces is extremely complicated to unravel. Detailed satellite measurements show that the average worldwide effect of clouds today is a slight net cooling, but nobody knows how cloud effects may change in the future.

- **Carbon Cycle.** The concentration of CO_2 in the atmosphere—the main driving force for climate change—is the result of many natural processes that cycle carbon between different forms. The process is akin to a busy highway, where the number of cars on the road is the balance of those entering and exiting. Some leave for a brief moment to refuel their engines and passengers, only to return quickly—just as vast quantities of CO_2 from the atmosphere are stored temporarily in plants during the growing season, only to return when the plants die. Most of the processes that shuttle carbon in and out of the atmosphere are sensitive to the amount of CO_2 already in the atmosphere. For example, some plants grow especially rapidly in elevated concentrations of carbon dioxide: as CO_2 rises, this "fertilization effect" could offset some of humanity's emissions, although field studies suggest that the availability of water and nutrients will dampen these effects. Nasty surprises also may be lurking within the carbon cycle. For example, if climate change causes less rainfall over the Amazon then massive fires in the drying forest could release still more carbon dioxide into the atmosphere and further dampen nature's ability to sop up excess CO_2 from the atmosphere. Although still speculative, this scenario is not implausible. The 1997–98 El Niño, for example, contributed to a widespread increase in forest fire activity in Southeast Asia and in South America.

• **Models of Global Climate.** What matters most in assessing the possible impacts of climate change on nature and human welfare are particular changes in rainfall, temperature, cloudiness, storms, and sundry other factors in particular locations, such as the wheat-growing region of Nebraska or the barrier islands at Cape Hatteras. A starting point for such assessments is models of the entire circulation of the atmosphere and the circulation of the oceans—called atmospheric general circulation models (GCMs) and oceanic GCMs. These models require vast amounts of data for calibration and presently occupy some of the world's largest supercomputers. Still, they are coarse in resolution: typical GCMs treat a roughly 100-by-100 kilometer area as a single unit, and thus they compute the same climate for Seattle as for Mount Rainier. (Experimental models, such as Japan's Earth Simulator, are yielding promising results running at a 10-by-10 km resolution.) To be tractable, GCMs must use simple mathematical parameters to approximate many complex processes, which is an additional source of predictive error. Some uncertainties and errors can propagate into large uncertainties when compounded over the multiple decades that are typical for GCM projections. GCMs have improved significantly in the last decade. Today's most complex models link atmosphere, oceans, biosphere, and human action; in the mid-1970s, by contrast, models usable for climate forecasting focused only on simple processes entirely within the atmosphere.

- **Abrupt Change.** Over the next few decades, the most likely impacts of climate change are within the realm of normal fluctuations in climate, such as changes in temperature, cloudiness, rainfall, and sea level. They are likely to unfold gradually and somewhat predictably, which will ease the task of adaptation. However, the forced change in Earth's heat balance caused by greenhouse gases might also yield abrupt and potentially catastrophic changes in climate, and there is ample evidence of such discontinuities in the past. Climate change could trigger alterations in the circulation of the oceans, which in turn might force a complete change in weather patterns, with unknown consequences. (Among the dramatic changes could be redirection in the Gulf Stream that, ironically, would make the North Atlantic region much colder.) There is strong evidence that the North Atlantic circulation has changed abruptly in the past when climate has cooled; the risk of such changes in a warming world are unknown. Already there is some evidence of potential changes in ocean circulation: parts of the Atlantic Ocean have become less salty since the 1950s, which is significant as it is changes in saltiness that, in part, determine the density of sea water and drive ocean circulation. Other nasty surprises may lurk in the warming of the Arctic tundra, which could release large amounts of methane (a strong greenhouse gas) presently locked away in ice crystals known as clathrates. Warmer temperatures might accelerate the normal movement and melting of the West Antarctic ice sheet; although presently thought to be well grounded, there is a small chance that the ice sheet could slide more rapidly into the ocean, which could raise sea levels by several meters over just a century. The likelihood of each of these events is difficult to assess but probably rises sharply with more rapid forcing of climate change; the full range of such catastrophic events is unknown.

- **Social Sciences and Humanities.** The fact that natural scientists have identified the problem of climate change as a physical phenomenon is not reason enough for policy response. Policy analysis also requires integrating insights from the social sciences, which has proved very difficult in practice. The greatest progress has been in integrating economics with physical assessments. These "integrated assessments" link a large number of different models and make it possible to assess the consequences of changing climate in the same units (dollars) as the cost of policies that could reduce climate change. However, this integration has left several major problems unsolved. Climate change involves costs and benefits that extend over long time periods—even generations. Standard techniques of discounting future costs and benefits into present values may be inappropriate when the consequences involve future generations whose preferences are unknown to today's generation of decision makers. Assessments also require integrating market costs and benefits—such as the impact of climate change on commodity crops—with effects that are difficult to measure in dollars. For example, how should we value unique species that go extinct when a changing climate erases their habitat? Surveys indicate that people are willing to pay large amounts to preserve some species (e.g., giant pandas) but not others; for many analysts, the existence of nature's biodiversity is reason enough to make every effort at protection. In addition, some types of assessments are politically charged. For example, poor nations that are less able to adapt are likely to suffer more greatly from climate change. However, wage levels are lower in these societies, which typically reduces the economic cost of lost life and health, thus lowering the estimated consequences of climate change. Similar results occur when the stress of heat is assessed— elderly populations suffer more than the young, but the elderly have fewer economically productive years left to lose. Studies built on such assumptions are typically assailed as unjust and politically untouchable. Which principles of justice should be applied if the average global consequences of changing climate are modest in the regions where societies are able to adapt easily, while highly adverse in areas already on the margin and unable to adjust? Quantitative assessments of the costs and benefits of climate policy rarely include any systematic treatment of politics, law, and institutions—despite the fact that these are organizing elements of society. These models may thus misstate societies' political choices and their ability to adapt to a changing climate, and they do a poor job of representing subtle processes such as the invention and application of new technologies.

All three of the policy options outlined in this memorandum envision substantial continued investment in the science of climate change so that future policy decisions will be better informed about the risks and costs of a changing climate. Regardless of the investment, however, it is likely that policy decisions today and in the future will have to be made in the context of extreme uncertainty. Moreover, the standard tools for making decisions under uncertainty are not easy to apply in this case. It may not be possible to hedge against some outcomes—such as extinctions or irreversible changes in climate—because species and climate are unique within our experience on Earth and we have no other planets with which to pool the risk. For some hazards, scientists have estimated the range of uncertainties; many other possible hazards are difficult to assess quantitatively or are simply unknown.

In 2002 President Bush established a new interagency, cabinet-level structure for managing U.S. investments in climate change science and technology. Within that structure, the Bush administration created the Climate Change Science Program (CCSP) and the Climate Change Technology Program (CCTP). We will discuss the CCTP later; the focus here is on the CCSP. Although government-wide efforts to ensure a rational and strategic investment in climate science date back to 1989, the CCSP's ten-year strategic research plan released in 2003 is the most comprehensive federal vision for climate science to date. It was based on unprecedented cooperation of federal agencies and adjusted through a detailed review process involving the NAS and other outside experts. The plan envisions support for better monitoring of the climate and seeks to study the causes of climate change; it includes a detailed strategy for investing in the support tools needed to aid policy decisions within the context of substantial uncertainty.

We think that this investment in science, which builds on earlier administrations' programs, is sound and requires no further attention from you at this point. However, we call your attention to three concerns.

First, you should know that the effectiveness of the government's investment in climate science will depend heavily on factors that are outside your direct control, such as the intellectual organization of the scientific effort. Over the last three decades the best climate models have become extremely complex and costly to maintain and run. Only a handful of models in the United States and a few others overseas operate at the most sophisticated frontier. With this small collection of highly complex tools, the scientific community must remain vigilant in ensuring that a diversity of approaches is supported and that efforts to compare model outputs do not yield "groupthink" that tends to overemphasize conventional wisdom while excluding fringe opinions and outliers that often spur substantial scientific insights.

Second, we find that the integration of social science and natural science modeling remains in its infancy. We are concerned that the social sciences are poorly organized to bring their insights to bear. Most assessments of climate change are based on quantitative models that make it difficult for most of the social sciences (except for economics) to participate in the debate. Policy analysis in this context is therefore framed in highly stylized "ideal" policies that do not account for how real policies are implemented by real political systems. That problem leaves you and your successors in the position of making policy choices with highly incomplete information about costs, benefits, and political consequences. For example, many of the models used to quantify the costs of controlling emissions assume that power plants fired with natural gas (which emits half the CO_2 per kilowatt of electricity from coal) or nuclear heat (which emits no CO_2) will be available when needed. Yet, in reality, the process of siting new power plants and their infrastructure such as reception facilities for imported liquefied natural gas (LNG) or disposal facilities for nuclear waste can be time consuming or impossible, which could raise the cost of efforts to control carbon. Political and legal experts have insights into these issues but, at present, are largely absent from the quantitative debate about environmental policy options.

Third, we note that the CCSP declares priorities but is strikingly silent on cost and value. The plan contains no estimates of cost, and the government's normal budgeting process focuses on an annual cycle that does not correspond with the CCSP's ten-year vision. The CCSP requires coordinating the actions of thirteen federal agencies and a complex multicommittee budget appropriation process in Congress that makes it difficult to move resources between agencies. Some aspects of climate science—such as building, launching, and operating satellites—are extremely expensive and dominate the total investment in climate science; NASA is the lead agency for most of those programs, and there is a danger that manned space flight and the new Moon/Mars initiative will crowd the budget for climate science. Overall, the grand vision of the CCSP is much larger than the budget available, which is a point underscored in the NAS's independent review of the CCSP.

We suggest that you direct your science adviser to convene a process to address these concerns. That process, which should include a prominent role for the NAS to help dispel any questions that "the science" is a handmaiden to politics, would ensure that the scientific community is organized to make optimal use of the increasingly costly climate monitoring and computer tools. It would also involve a more active effort to assess the value of different scientific research programs for policy decisions, which would ease the task of setting research priorities. In fourteen years of attempts to create an integrated federal budget and strategy for climate change, there has never been a serious effort to compare systematically the declared priorities of scientists and policymakers, a sober assessment of investment value, and actual budgetary spending. Yet the size of total spending on climate research is approaching $2 billion per year; future policymakers could benefit substantially from a more rational budgeting strategy.

ADAPTING TO A CHANGING CLIMATE

The impact of a changing climate on American interests depends on the consequences that are likely to occur and the ease with which we can adapt. Your assessment of these factors will influence your policy strategy. If you think we are largely immune and highly adaptive, then the case for controlling greenhouse gas emissions is weakened and your policy strategy might focus on boosting America's adaptive capacity. If you are skeptical of our ability to adapt then the need to address the root cause of climate change—emissions of greenhouse gases—becomes more urgent.

The most comprehensive assessment of climate impacts on the United States is the "National Assessment of the Potential Consequences of Climate Variability and Change," produced as part of the 1990 Global Change Research Act and completed in 2000. (Please see the Overview Conclusions reproduced in Appendix B.) The report assessed climate impacts during the course of this century in five climate-sensitive sectors, such as agriculture and coastal zones, across twenty different regions of the United States. The "National Assessment" complements a global assessment of climate impacts completed the same year by the IPCC.

The report concluded that it is highly likely that rising sea levels will cause erosion and some inundation of coastal wetlands. (Sea level rises because water expands when it warms; in addition, the runoff from melting glaciers raises the volume of water in the oceans.) Warmer winter temperatures are also likely to reduce snowpack, causing difficulties for watershed management in regions where water resources are already tapped heavily, such as in California and the Colorado River basin. Alaska is likely to face special difficulties since many roads and pipelines are built on permafrost, which is a poor foundation when it thaws. Across much of the United States higher heat indexes and more frequent heat waves are also likely, which will impose the need to build electric power systems that can meet the greater demand for air conditioning. Not all the news is bad, however. The study finds that agriculture and forestry are likely to benefit from higher concentrations of CO_2 (which causes plants to grow more rapidly if water and nutrients are ample). Growing stress from heat and drought could be harmful, especially to natural ecosystems that are less able to adapt than those that are actively managed by humans, such as crops. The impacts of changing climate are likely to vary considerably across regions.

For example, farmers already working at the edge of the climatic zone for their crops will likely face the need to switch crops or face losses. Soybean farming in the already warm southeastern United States is likely to suffer, but new areas for cultivation may open in the far north where temperatures are presently too low for soybeans. Under most scenarios, the National Assessment concludes that U.S. farmers and consumers would benefit from higher crop yields and lower prices. Other studies, however, suggest that some farmers—especially those without access to irrigation—could lose under many plausible scenarios of climate change.

In assessing the sources and impacts of climate change it is important to be mindful that much else is changing on the planet at the same time. Even as the "anthrosphere" in which the human economy operates is becoming more adaptive to climate, humanity is also imposing substantial changes on the energy, nutrient, and water cycles of nature's biosphere. Deforestation, planting crops, paving, building, and other changes in the land will affect nature's ability to adjust to the buildup of greenhouse gases. The fragmentation of natural forest ecosystems, for example, probably makes nature less adaptive because it impedes migration with the changing climate.

Over time, the United States and most other advanced industrialized countries have become more immune to variations in climate. In 1850 about two-thirds of the U.S. economy depended on the climate; farming, forestry, hunting and fishing, and other "outdoors" activities are vulnerable to climate change. Today, only about 5 percent of U.S. economic activity is affected directly by climate, although perhaps about one-third of total economic output has a significant indirect link to climate. A large and increasing fraction of the economy is largely decoupled from climate and weather. We live in office buildings with climate control, fly in aircraft that land and take off in nearly zero visibility, and buy food and other products on a world market that increasingly locates production where weather and other factors are most favorable. In contrast, less wealthy communities—both the poor here in the United

States and the very poor in the developing world—are generally more vulnerable and less able to adapt.

Despite better climate-proofing, we are not invulnerable. Estimates compiled by the National Oceanic and Atmospheric Administration (NOAA) suggest that on average severe weather events cause $11 billion in damages per year nationally. In outlier years, which may become more common with climate change, single storms have caused billions of dollars in damage. The assessed value of coastal real estate between Miami and Palm Beach alone is about $1 trillion; much of its value is tied to the proximate ocean and thus vulnerable as the water rises.

Some policy responses can boost our adaptive capacity in anticipation of a changing climate. For example, investment in better weather and climate forecasting has already reduced vulnerabilities to El Niño, a natural climatic cycle that typically occurs every two to five years and affects the whole planet. It is associated with extreme weather in the United States and causes crops to fail in Australia, Indonesia, and elsewhere in southern Asia. The 1982–83 El Niño, the strongest on record, caused abnormally high water levels on the Colorado River that threatened the integrity of the Glen Canyon dam, situated immediately above the Grand Canyon; failure of that dam, or others stressed by high water flows, could cause massive loss of life. The 1997–98 El Niño, also strong by historical standards, caused $4.5 billion in total losses of crops and property in the United States alone.

Over the last fifteen years governments and the private sector have developed sophisticated weather forecasting tools that can now assign a reasonable probability for the onset of El Niño a year in advance, making it possible to adjust water usage and crop choices, purchase grain for storage, and adopt changes in technology and behavior that can ameliorate El Niño's impact. Recently developed technologies for correcting errors in climate models hold the promise of two-year predictability for El Niño events. Equally important to the creation of early-warning systems is the promotion of flexibility, such as efficient markets that reliably price the scarcity of water. All of these measures to dampen the effect of El Niño on modern economies have occurred quite apart from the threat of climate change, and except in the poorest regions they are likely to spread widely in the coming decades. Other early-warning and adaptive responses have also limited the damage from other weather-related hazards, such as tornadoes, intense storms, drought, and flood.

As president you will be hard pressed to identify many ways that the federal government can effectively accelerate the "climate proofing" of our society. Most of the growing immunity to climate is the result of normal economic development rather than active policy. However, we highlight three areas where you might consider further action. First, you may want to make additional efforts to ensure that potential future climate impacts are known by those whose actions, today, could ease future adaptation. The need for information is especially great in the planning and construction of costly, long-lived infrastructure, such as bridges, power plants, and water-treatment plants located in coastal zones where sea level will rise. Already much is underway. River managers are examining the risk that saltwater from higher seas might reach the public water supply intakes in cities such as Philadelphia and Sacramento. When Boston city planners revamped that city's waterfront in the 1980s, they allowed for a rise in sea level in the design for new sea walls and protection against storm surges. Compared with just a decade ago, most new large weather-sensitive infrastructures in the United States are planned with an eye toward long-term climate change.

Second, and related, is the need to promote institutions that will aid adaptation. Many such institutions already exist, such as agricultural futures markets that aid in the hedging of risks and encourage actors in the private sector to gain the information they need about climate and weather impacts. Agricultural and water markets still fall far short of their efficient ideal, however. In the American West, especially, a plethora of distortions keep water from flowing to the places where it could yield the greatest economic value. In agriculture, the 2002 Farm Act probably set back the cause of creating an adaptive farm sector by reinvigorating a highly subsidized scheme that centrally determines crop choices and by exacerbating distortions in the value of farm land. The Bush administration has announced its intention to roll back that farm program if the European Union were to make similar cuts in subsidies; that deal is entangled in the foundering talks on the next trade round in the WTO. The long-term U.S. interest in making the agricultural sector even more adaptive is additional reason to pursue such a deal—quite apart from saving billions of dollars per year in price supports and removing distortions that propagate harm throughout world trade in agricultural products.

Third, many countries will press the United States to be accountable for the effects of climate change in other countries, notably in the developing world where exposure to climate is greater and the ability to adapt is already thin. In India, for example, despite a thriving industrial and service sector, roughly one-quarter of economic output and two-thirds of all employment are linked to agriculture. The United States could invest in programs to assist these countries in adapting, such as by helping them to build modern weather forecasting systems, with particular emphasis on improved forecasting of extreme weather hazards. But the track record with these programs is mixed, in part because it is very difficult to isolate "adaptation" projects from the broader development of the whole economy. An alternative approach is not to invest in adaptation-specific projects at all, but to assist these countries with their normal process of economic development. Wealthier and more democratic societies are generally better able to adapt on their own. Famine tends to arrive more readily when unaccountable tyrants govern the land.

It is probably not possible to achieve complete invulnerability to a changing climate. Three types of impacts on humanity, in particular, may be difficult to manage. If you assign importance to these hazards then it will be hard to justify a policy that relies mainly on adaptation to a changing climate rather than controlling emissions and mitigating the climate problem at its root.

First, some countries—mainly developing countries—will face enormous difficulty adapting. Low-lying nations, such as the archipelago of Vanuatu in the Pacific and Bangladesh, large swaths of which sit barely one meter above sea level, face the specter of disaster if sea levels rise. In Bangladesh alone, more than ten million people live within one meter of sea level. Economically, it may be much less costly to move these populations (or ignore their troubles), but as a matter of justice and politics that option may not be viable.

Second, some climate hazards may not readily confine themselves outside U.S. borders. For example, many scientists have suggested that a warmer and wetter climate will facilitate the spread of malaria, yellow fever, and other water-borne diseases. Industrialized countries have already brought these diseases under control, and developing countries will probably do the same as they become wealthier. It may prove difficult, however, to check the spread of climate-linked diseases as borders become more porous. When the United States brought malaria under control one hundred years ago, it was difficult for malarial patients to travel and reinfect a zone; today, every major malarial zone in the world is less than twenty-four hours from the United States by airplane, and forty million international air passengers arrive in the United States every year. Unlike property risks, for which insurance markets can respond rapidly to a change in danger, risks to human lives create liabilities that require a whole generation for adjustment. The 1999 outbreak in New York of the West Nile virus—a disease carried in birds that is transmitted by mosquito in a manner similar to malaria—illustrated the dangers and underscored that the public is easily panicked. The virus is known to have infected sixty-two people that year in New York State and killed seven; it has since spread across much of the United States. Combating health effects may require improvements in public health systems and disease monitoring, including outside the United States. Such investments are already rising in priority as we contemplate responding to possible bioterrorism attacks.

Third, and finally, it may be extremely difficult to adapt to the consequences of abrupt climate changes—such as a rapid shift in circulation in the North Atlantic or an accelerated century-long melting of the West Antarctic ice sheet. Better monitoring and analysis of these scenarios could improve our adaptive capacity, but the dislocations could be so large that adaptation is not an option.

Of these three points of vulnerability, the third could affect U.S. interests and security most dramatically. Yet the risks are difficult to quantify. We expect that such abrupt climate changes—perhaps low in probability but drastic in consequences for society—will become an ever larger part of the public debate about how to respond to climate change. If the public becomes worried about these scenarios it will be difficult to respond with a policy that relies mainly on adaptation.

CONTROLLING EMISSIONS

Whether and how you adopt policies to control emissions of greenhouse gases will be politically the most visible and contro-versial aspect of your climate change policy strategy. Since 1988, prominent senators and members of Congress have introduced bills to require mandatory limits on emissions, although not one of those bills has passed. In 2003, the Senate voted on a bill sponsored by Senators Joe Lieberman (D-CT) and John McCain (R-AZ), which would have imposed caps on U.S. emissions of green-house gases. The measure attracted forty-three positive votes— "free votes," say its detractors, who never expected the bill to pass, but for many others the near majority was a sign of grow-ing legislative interest in adopting some sort of binding limits on emissions. Before the vote on the McCain-Lieberman bill, the only other time that the full Senate has voted on climate policy was in July 1997, four months before the final negotiations for the Kyoto Protocol, when the Senate passed the Byrd-Hagel resolution by a vote of 95-0, declaring that the Senate would not accept any treaty that did not hold developing countries to the same commitment schedules as the United States. (We address this nonbinding res-olution in more detail later.)

Absent mandatory controls, since 1994 the federal government has had in place a program to encourage private firms to make voluntary reductions—also known as "1605(b)" after the section of the Energy Policy Act of 1992. In 2002, 228 American firms claimed that they achieved reductions totaling 265 million metric tons of CO_2 equivalents (about 4 percent of actual gross U.S. emissions that year). Many firms have participated in 1605(b) because they see it as a way to gain public credit for cost-effective reductions that they would have made anyway. Many participants also appear to believe that acknowledged reductions will also lead to future rewards, such as extra emission credits in some future emission trading program.

Critics complain that the voluntary 1605(b) program has loose accounting standards. (Some of that critique will be blunted by new accounting rules presently under development.) In recent years, several states have begun their own programs to register emission reductions and to encourage firms to measure their emission of greenhouse gases; those programs generally have much tighter accounting standards than 1605(b). Some observers nonetheless are critical of all these "voluntary" schemes because insofar as they offer an implicit promise to recognize emission reductions, they are, in effect, a back-door strategy for implementing a soft cap on emissions. These critics argue that government should not reward incumbent firms just because they file paperwork to register low-cost emission cuts that they would have made anyway. Alternative methods for allocating rewards such as a binding emission trading system could be much more efficient. For example, an auction of permits would deliver the value created in these permits to the public owners of the atmosphere rather than to private firms that are talented at filling out forms.

Designing Effective Emission Controls

Crafting a strategy for controlling emissions is a complicated and potentially risky task because it involves altering the metabolism of the industrial economy, which depends on fossil fuels. Over

[27]

the last decade, successive administrations have examined four broad types of policies.

First, the government could make fuller use of voluntary programs. In addition to 1605(b), the government could make more aggressive use of labeling and informational programs. For example, the "Energy Star" program of the Department of Energy (DOE) and the Environmental Protection Agency (EPA) has had some success in convincing manufacturers to produce more efficient electrical equipment. For example, computer monitors, VCRs, and other devices used to consume large amounts of power in "standby" mode; "Energy Star" has helped to reduce this parasitic consumption of power without much altering the functionality of equipment. Manufacturers have been keen to participate as that allows them to show the "Energy Star" logo on their products, and this "voluntary" approach has probably forestalled less flexible binding regulations. Without such programs, few consumers would have been able to determine on their own why their electricity bills were so high and to identify viable technological alternatives.

Many voluntary programs have focused on household energy decisions. All told, about one-third of U.S. emissions of carbon dioxide come from households, and there is ample evidence that households are especially far from the frontier of best practice in their usage of energy. Homeowners often do not invest in even in the simplest and most cost-effective measures, such as adding insulation and buying efficient appliances. Many voluntary programs directed at homeowners already exist, but it will be difficult for the federal government to exert much additional direct leverage since many of the key decisions rest with state policymakers and regulators. For example, many states with regulated power utilities have allowed (or even mandated) utilities to work with customers to find cost-effective ways to provide energy services (such as lighting and heating) while also limiting demand for electricity and gas. These "demand-side management" programs have been inspired by the logic that it is often much less costly for society to invest in energy efficiency than to expand energy supply systems. Yet the actual record of these programs is mixed. Some have been highly successful—especially those involving large energy users (e.g., substituting ultra-efficient heat pumps for traditional air conditioners) and those that require only simple changes in end technologies (e.g., substituting efficient compact fluorescent lamps that provide the same light output while consuming one-quarter the electricity and lasting ten times longer than the incandescent bulbs that they replace). Although the logic of these programs is compelling and there is a history of notable achievements, in many cases these programs have been justified with accounting methods that regulators have allowed but that would not pass normal market tests.

An expanded voluntary effort should include not just attention to emissions from the energy system but also changes in the use of land, which could help reduce the roughly one-quarter of world greenhouse gas emissions that come from tropical deforestation. You could endorse efforts such as those of an international coalition of leading American and European nongovernmental organizations (NGOs)—the Climate, Community, and Biodiversity Alliance—which has developed voluntary standards for projects that limit carbon while also helping to preserve biological diversity and improve local livelihoods. To date, such voluntary programs have not played a central part in the U.S. government's efforts to promote emission controls. You could also redouble federal diplomatic and financial support for programs that build on existing U.S.-led diplomatic initiatives such as the Congo Basin Forest Partnership that links key governments and NGOs in West Africa with the goal of protecting forests and other natural resources in order to improve people's standard of living in that region.

Second, you could develop a policy of controlling emissions through direct regulation, such as mandatory energy efficiency standards. Already government imposes many energy efficiency standards; their effectiveness and economic merits are hotly contested, but the potential to raise efficiency is substantial. For example, in 1972 the average U.S. refrigerator consumed 1,800 kilowatt hours (kWh) per year. Through a series of binding standards—

first in California and then nationwide—power consumption by the average refrigerator has declined to about 500 kWh per year, even as refrigerators have swelled in size and functionality has increased with the addition of such features as automatic defrost. It is difficult to disentangle the effect of higher electricity prices, awareness of energy issues, and autonomous innovation within the refrigerator business from the specific effect of tightening efficiency standards, but many experts argue that such standards are proof that government can and should force technological change through binding rules on equipment suppliers.

The single largest effect of government energy efficiency standards on total energy consumption and emissions of greenhouse gases is in personal vehicles. Ever since 1975 the United States has set standards that require each major vehicle manufacturer to achieve a minimum average level of efficiency for the fleet of cars and light trucks it sells—the so-called Corporate Average Fuel Economy (CAFE) standards. These standards, along with higher gasoline prices, explain why during the 1980s total fuel consumed (and carbon emitted) from personal vehicles actually declined even as the total distance traveled by passenger cars and trucks rose steadily every year. Only in the 1990s did emissions resume their rise—partly because the efficiency standards for new cars have been largely stagnant since 1985 and notably because new consumer tastes favor less efficient "light trucks" over "passenger cars." The CAFE rules treat these categories as distinct and allow much lower mileage averages for trucks (20.7 miles per gallon, or mpg) than for cars (27.5 mpg). (The National Highway Traffic Safety Administration, which administers the CAFE program, has raised light truck standards to 22.2 mpg for the model year 2007.) The category of "light trucks" includes nearly all minivans, crossover vehicles such as DaimlerChrysler's PT Cruiser, and all SUVs; today, 36 percent of registered vehicles are "light trucks." Roughly 5 percent of personal vehicle sales are trucks that weigh more than 8,500 pounds and therefore are not even subject to the relatively lax fuel economy standards for light trucks; favorable treatment under federal tax laws creates additional incentives for people to use such ultra-heavy personal machines.

In 2002 the National Research Council issued a report showing that it was possible to increase fuel economy for new passenger cars and trucks by about 50 percent over the next decade, with little impact on vehicle safety. It also recommended eliminating the bureaucratic distinction between "cars" and "light trucks," which is a vestige of much earlier policies that aimed to protect U.S. light truck manufacturers from foreign competition and to exempt short-haul industrial and farm vehicles from the strict fuel economy standards for passenger cars. The logic of that earlier era is difficult to justify today.

We find, however, that most firms and economists are united in their belief that product- and facility-specific regulation—often called "command and control" regulation—is excessively costly. For example, strict energy efficiency standards force consumers to spend capital on efficiency features that they otherwise would not select; more costly vehicles cause consumers to delay purchases, which in turn probably makes the vehicle fleet older and perhaps less efficient than it would be otherwise. However, such regulation may be your only option if citizens abhor policies that raise the price of carbon-rich fuels.

Third, you could pursue a market-based policy that relies on taxing emissions—often called a "carbon tax" since carbon dioxide is the main greenhouse gas. The tax sends a price signal to firms and households, encouraging them to reduce emissions where that would be cost effective. As economic policy it is attractive because with a tax you will know the cost that your policy imposes on the economy; unlike a cap on emissions (which we discuss below), there is little risk that your policy could accidentally impose a cost on the economy that is higher than Americans are willing to pay. Revenues from a carbon tax could be used to lighten taxes on capital or labor, which could help to accelerate economic growth; tax revenues could also be earmarked for special purposes such as research and development (R&D) into climate-friendly technology and other politically useful activities.

The central problem with this approach is its political difficulty. The last presidential effort to create a broad-based tax on fossil fuels was the Clinton administration's ill-fated "BTU tax" that was part of its 1993 economic recovery package. Although the proposed tax was very small (about four cents per gallon of gasoline, which is much less than the typical variation in fuel prices during the summer driving season), many voters disliked the measure and Congress declined to pass it. The conventional wisdom that has arisen from that debacle is that direct regulation and alternative policy instruments that impose costs with stealth while visibly demonstrating action are politically more likely to succeed than higher taxes. The failure of the BTU tax, however, also stemmed from the failure of the Clinton administration to articulate a compelling special purpose that would require the energy tax.

Given the public's assumed reluctance to pay higher taxes, it will be difficult to muster the political coalition needed to adopt a carbon energy tax. Moreover, nearly all environmental groups actively reject the tax approach because its effect on emissions is uncertain. Instead, they prefer emission caps, which make it clear what the economy must deliver for the environment.

In addition to the political arithmetic that has deterred U.S. policymakers from seriously considering carbon taxes, such measures also present special problems for international coordination. If you impose a meaningful tax on the United States you will want to ensure that other countries impose similar measures on their firms as well. In practice, though, countries that have adopted carbon taxes typically riddle them with loopholes and special exceptions to reward politically powerful groups and to reduce the real costs of compliance. A coordinated international approach based on taxation would require complementary rules to limit these loopholes, and such rules would be difficult to enforce. Indeed, similar types of disciplines on tax policy exist in the WTO, where despite sophisticated enforcement institutions it has been very difficult to assure compliance.

The problems with the preceding policy options have led most analysts and politicians to focus on a fourth option: a market-based "cap-and-trade" system. In this scheme, each nation would adopt a binding cap on its total emissions. The nation would then allocate emission credits within its borders—probably far "upstream," at power plants, refineries, and other primary users of fossil fuels that cause emissions of greenhouse gases. (A "downstream" system could be costly to administer since millions of firms and households, each causing relatively low emissions, would be required to engage in the trading system.) Firms would then be free to trade these credits, which would ensure that actual emission controls are applied where it is cheapest. The United States has successfully used such "cap-and-trade" systems in phasing out lead in gasoline and in controlling emissions of sulfur dioxide, the leading cause of acid rain. This vision for a cap-and-trade system is already built into the Kyoto Protocol, mainly because of the insistence of the Clinton administration. It is also a central part of domestic policy proposals such as the McCain-Lieberman bill.

An emission trading system offers opportunity for political arbitrage. The permits that would be allocated under this system could be extremely valuable, and special handouts could be used to blunt opposition and reward politically powerful constituencies while not actually appearing as a cost on the government's books. When Congress crafted the 1990 Clean Air Act, it awarded most of the sulfur emission credits to existing emitters, the interest group that would have been most adamant in opposing emission controls. Studies show that awarding just 10 percent of carbon emission permits to the hardest-hit stakeholders—coal mining firms in particular—could blunt their opposition by offsetting their immediate losses as the economy shifts away from carbon-intensive fuels. We question the economic efficiency of a scheme that diverts large resources to an ailing industry—rather than allowing the market itself to determine coal's fate—but as a matter of political expediency such allocations are probably unavoidable. Your economic advisers will urge you to auction the permits, as is done in many other areas in which the government leases a public good for private purposes (e.g., the radio spectrum for cell phones). Using standard methods for calculating the value of property rights, the stock of U.S. emission credits could be worth about $1 trillion, making this the largest allocation of public property since the opening of the American West.

Several entities have already created pilot programs to trade credits and prove the merit of the concept. For example, the Chicago Climate Exchange (CCX) opened in December 2003 for trading among nineteen North American entities that have agreed to reduce their emissions 1 percent per year for four years to demonstrate the functionality of the market. At present, carbon dioxide permits are trading in CCX on a spot basis for less than $1 per ton—an extremely low level that reflects the lack of any meaningful incentive to control emissions in the U.S. economy. Similar pilot efforts are taking shape in the northeastern United States. The European Union has created a binding trading system for large industrial sources that will begin operation in 2005.

In principle, the greatest gains from emission trading will arise in an international system. Indeed, the architects of the Kyoto Protocol envisioned that the thirty-eight industrialized countries with binding emission caps would be allowed to trade portions of their emission quotas on an international exchange. As you evaluate whether such a system is in the U.S. interest we urge you to develop a careful strategy for assessing which nations should be allowed inside an international trading system that includes the United States.

On the one hand, it is useful to involve as many countries as possible in the trading system because that offers the greatest potential gains from trade. Economic modeling and pilot projects have already proved that flexibility in the geography of emission control can cut costs dramatically. For example, American Electric Power—the largest coal-burning U.S. electric utility—has demonstrated that it is less costly to limit net emissions to the atmosphere by protecting a rainforest in Bolivia than to control emissions from its existing power plants located in the United States. Gas companies in western Europe and pipeline companies in Japan are exploring ways to get credit for investing in less-leaky pipelines and more efficient compressors on the gas transmission system in Russia. Gazprom, Russia's natural gas monopoly, welcomes this approach because it would attract badly needed investment in its crumbling gas-transmission system, and the Western firms see it as an opportunity to enter the Russian gas market and control emissions at much lower cost than in the already tight and relatively efficient systems they operate at home.

On the other hand, the countries that have the greatest opportunity for low-cost emission controls—developing countries, as well as Russia and Ukraine—are those that have the weakest internal institutions and thus are least likely to be able to monitor and enforce the system. Since emission credits are analogous to a new form of currency, countries with weak institutions could print excessive quantities of this new currency, degrading the value of the scrip held by all others and causing higher emissions that undermine the scheme's environmental objectives. An international treaty probably does not offer strong enough institutions to deter such actions; violators could be ejected, but by the time their transgressions were known for certain it might be too late for others to adjust their behavior before the currency scheme unravels. No durable currency has ever sprung forth by starting with large numbers of highly diverse agents in the absence of strong institutions that are essential to assuring the integrity of the currency. It is useful to keep in mind the experience in Europe of creating the euro. In that case, twelve countries created a common currency within an existing context of strong collective institutions, independent courts, a robust administrative bureaucracy, and a new central bank. Even then, the transition has been far from seamless. In 2003, when France and Germany failed to comply with limits on their budget deficits, the European Monetary Union declined to penalize them, even though this failure in essence siphoned value from compliant members. It would be a daunting task to attempt to create a currency of emission credits in the context of much weaker international law with the participation of countries such as Russia and most of the developing nations that question the need for any emission controls.

The analogy with creating a currency suggests that it may be better to build a market from the "bottom up" rather than attempt to create an international trading system with centralized Kyoto-style rules that work "top down." Countries that care most about the environmental problem at hand would establish their own trading systems (currencies) and enforcement rules. Then portals (exchanges) between the systems would be established according to bilateral consent. Thus countries could control their exposures to poor enforcement and excessive allocation by deciding where they open portals. Inspired by the early years of the General Agreement on Tariffs and Trade (GATT), members in this bottom-up regime might also create international rules of mutual recognition, reciprocity, and most-favored-nation arrangements to ensure that those who accept the strictures of core trading arrangements gain the benefit of access to all markets that are part of the regime. Enforcement would rest principally with member states and the market, which would value each country's scrip individually, just as currency markets assign varying values to dollars, yen, euros, and rupees.

This bottom-up approach cannot be sustained forever. As the screws are tightened you must have a credible plan for eventually involving all emitters so that none can "free ride" on the benefits of protecting the climate while paying none of the cost. As the number of parties grows there will be a need for better central coordination and multilateral enforcement systems. But that topic might be deferred until some future moment when the foundations for a broader system have been laid and tested. Indeed, the architects of GATT did not create any provisions for multilateral enforcement; a system of "dispute panels" arose later within the GATT system. Only today, more than fifty years after the modest creation of GATT, has an effective enforcement system arisen through experience, learning, and the creation of institutional arrangements such as the WTO.

Your view of the urgency of the climate problem will shape how you strike this balance between including many nations versus starting with a small number of like-minded countries that already have strong institutions in place. If you think that substantial controls on emissions are necessary and urgent, then a global approach involving most or all nations is important since you must rapidly gain leverage over the majority of world emissions. If you think that we have several decades (or longer) to develop an effective global emission control system, then you can afford to pursue a policy strategy that starts with modest coverage and limits on emissions and then evolves from the bottom up.

The credibility of efforts to create a trading system probably matters much more than the exact stringency and timing of cuts. There are long lead times in shifting energy systems; delay today creates the possibility to gather more information and wait until new technologies are available, but delay also carries costs of lost opportunity if investors ignore the possibility of strict future limits. In the developing world, where energy systems are expanding rapidly and equipment purchased today will condition technology opportunities for decades, there may be a special need for credible decisions now that send a long-term signal for change.

The Cost of Controlling Emissions

Even if you employ a well-designed market-based system of emission trading there are many potential economic risks in the magnitude and timing of the cut. Modest cuts in emissions, such as a 5 percent to 10 percent cut below the trajectory of emissions over a decade or longer, probably pose few risks for the economy. Firms and households will respond with low-cost, minor changes in technology and practice; an emission trading system will allow flexibility in exactly where the economy makes the reduction.

The timing of deeper cuts, however, requires greater care. Roughly half of U.S. emissions come from capital stock, such as power plants and steel mills, that has a lifetime of approximately twenty-five years or longer. This stock turns over slowly. Tight limits imposed with little warning over a short period could require the owners to implement costly retrofits or abandon these facilities. Yet such premature retirement of capital equipment would offer few environmental benefits, since the climate change problem itself is caused by the slow accumulation of greenhouse gases in the atmosphere. The amount of warming is more sensitive to the trajectory of emissions over time than to the exact timing of emission controls.

There are no precise maps to guide your decisions on the timing and cost of emission controls. The Clinton administration commissioned two studies through the Department of Energy on this issue and received diametrically opposed answers. One, a survey of national laboratories, found that many emission control technologies were already available for substantial emission cuts; a vigorous national commitment to energy efficiency, it argued, could keep emissions at approximately 1990 levels for little cost. The other relied on macroeconomic models and suggested that complying with the Kyoto commitments could cost hundreds of billions of dollars. Other studies using similar methods also concluded that this high cost yielded little benefit of averted climate change. This discrepancy reflects, in part, a conflict between the intellectual paradigms that guide the experts. Engineers who look at energy systems piece by piece find waste aplenty; optimally designed projects and technologies, they claim, will allow firms and households to save money while also cutting emissions. Economists tend to see the economy as an equilibrium that is costly to disturb; even if money-saving potentials exist, they claim, it may be costly to gather the information needed to identify and implement the best measures within the real organizations that populate the economy. Efforts to combine these two perspectives have proved difficult but generally suggest that considerable carbon savings are available at low cost. In 2000 the Clinton administration's DOE published a comprehensive scenario analysis of the U.S. economy. It concluded that the expected level of emissions in 2010 could be cut by 5 percent with fuller implementation of money-saving energy efficiency projects. Nonetheless, the study showed that emissions would rise overall in the absence of policies that, in effect, raised the price of carbon emissions.

We note that long-lived capital assets are typically much more responsive to policy incentives than suggested by their old name-plates. The White House, for example, is two centuries old; yet throughout the building you find modern conveniences and energy-efficient equipment, from computers to refrigerators, that were unavailable when John and Abigail Adams took up residence in 1800. The nation's oldest fossil fuel power plants that are connected to the grid date to the 1920s, but inside their brick walls the facilities have little in common with flapper-era technology. We also note that those who have argued that rapid and deep emission cuts are feasible often fail to recognize that technologies do not automatically appear where they are needed. Rather, technological change is often encumbered by the organizations and networks that must evolve alongside any transformation of the whole energy system.

The pace at which policy can encourage lower emissions is revealed in passenger and freight transportation, which accounts for about one-quarter of all U.S. emissions of greenhouse gases. Beyond the ten- to fifteen-year lifetime of new cars, another five years is typically needed to develop a new line of products, and still longer is required for testing and acceptance of truly radical new technologies. Ultra-efficient hybrid-engine vehicles, for example, first appeared on the U.S. market in 1999, yet four years later they accounted for only 0.3 percent of new vehicles sold and a much smaller fraction of the total passenger miles driven in the United States.

As a rule, complete transformation of the energy system takes about five decades. The shift to automobiles as the dominant mode of transportation in the United States required building new infrastructure (roads), head-to-head competition with the incumbents (rail cars and horses), and a complete shift in fueling systems from solid coal and hay to liquid oil-based products. Few pondered in the 1880s—when personal cars entered the U.S. market as leisure toys for the super-rich—the slow pace of diffusion of automobile technology or how pervasive automobiles would eventually become. The New York vehicle census found that cars outnumbered horses for the first time only in 1912—and New York's rich population was at the forefront of this transportation revolution. (Today, ironically, the super-rich have reverted to horses for leisure.) We are also mindful that analysts often overstate the potential of new technologies, forgetting that for every transformation traced to an original technological seed there have been dozens of false starts, such as Ford's amphibious car that promised to allow seamless interconnection between road and waterway mobility.

If you impose an excessively tight cap on U.S. emissions, you could repeat the experience with Kyoto in which an unrealistic cap forced the United States to consider either a politically unrealistic shell game of purchasing credits from Russia or simply exiting the regime. One solution to this problem is to create a "safety valve" in the trading system—a mechanism that allows the government to issue additional emission credits at an agreed price. In effect, this "valve" would limit the price of the emission credits and would make a cap-and-trade system behave like a tax if the cost of compliance rose higher than expected—if, for example, firms did not have enough time to meet a stringent cap on emissions with the normal turnover of the capital stock. Critics of the "safety valve," however, argue that only the terror of potentially high prices will force firms to focus on low-carbon innovations.

In developing your climate strategy you should be aware that many gases trap heat and cause changes in climate. Carbon dioxide is a relatively weak gas, but it is emitted in such prodigious quantities that it accounts for most of the current and expected future change in climate. Methane, by contrast, is a much stronger greenhouse gas, but the volume emitted is tiny compared with CO_2. Whereas CO_2 lingers a century or so in the atmosphere, methane survives in the atmosphere for just a decade. Thus efforts to control methane will have a rapid effect on climate but little impact on the long term. Avoiding carbon dioxide emissions is essential to long-term climate protection, but decades are required for the atmosphere to "feel" effects of changing the trajectory of carbon emissions. Scientists have developed indexes that account for these different properties of gases, allowing for crude conversion of different gases into common units—typically measured in "CO_2 equivalents."

In 2002, the gross U.S. emission of greenhouse gases totaled 6.9 billion metric tons of CO_2 equivalents. Of that total, 83 percent was emitted as CO_2 itself; the rest was as methane (9 percent), nitrous oxide (6 percent), and other gases (2 percent). Offsetting those gross emissions was the absorption of CO_2 by U.S. forests and croplands, with estimates ranging as high as one billion tons of CO_2. (Nobody is quite sure how much carbon is absorbed on U.S. territory. Some studies suggest that the quantity is extremely large because U.S. forests are still rebounding from massive deforestation in the nineteenth century, which implies that current high absorption is merely a transient effect.)

In principle, any effort to control emissions should set broad goals and then leave firms and households to find the emissions that are least costly to control. For example, firms such as the sanitation giant Waste Management have discovered that it is inexpensive to control methane from landfills by adopting new technologies to contain and manage landfill gas. The gas is so rich in methane—which is also the main ingredient in natural gas—that the landfill managers have been able to sell it for a profit. By encouraging the search for such innovative low-cost solutions, a multi-gas strategy can be less costly than policies that focus on just one gas (e.g., CO_2) or even on just one activity (e.g., emissions from large electric power plants). In practice, however, many of these gases and activities are difficult to monitor, and thus you must balance the hypothetical benefits of a multi-gas comprehensive approach against the cost and difficulty of its administration. Faced with exactly this challenge, the European Union, which is developing the world's first international system for trading emission credits, has opted initially to restrict the system just to easily measured CO_2 from burning fossil fuels at industrial sources. The EU system regulates other sources and gases separately and establishes a plan to include them in the trading system at a later date, when monitoring of emissions has improved and the trading system has proved its mettle.[2]

Finally, the metrics that are used to measure progress could have a large impact on the cost of compliance and the success of attempts to engage other countries in a collective effort to limit emissions. In most countries, and in the Kyoto process, goals have been set in terms of the volume of emissions—tons of CO_2 equivalents per year. Those terms often make the United States look like a poor performer, as we account for about one-quarter of the world's total emissions, which is hardly surprising since the United States also accounts for about one-quarter of the world's economic activity. The second-largest emitter (China) is quite far behind, at only 13 percent. After that follow Russia (7 percent), Japan (5 percent), and India (4 percent), and then many others spaced close together. Individual European nations account for small shares; the twenty-five nations of the EU collectively, however, account for less than one-sixth of the world's emissions.

Volumetric measures are also problematic as instruments for policy because they leave the United States and other countries exposed to unintended consequences. Over the short term, the single greatest factor in determining emissions in the United States has been the size of the economy; when the U.S. economy grew

---

[2]Regarding multi-gas strategies, you should be aware that a controversy is brewing within the scientific community about the role of soot in climate change. Emitted from diesel engines, biomass burning, power generation (mainly by coal), and other activities, soot can absorb heat and cause climate warming. Soot particles also accelerate the formation of clouds, but as mentioned earlier the exact effects of clouds on climate remains an area of ongoing scientific dispute. The soot debate is unlikely to alter the fundamental theory of climate change, but if soot proves to be a major cause of climate change then the allocation of responsibility by nation and activity may change a bit. Developing countries may account for a disproportionate share of the soot flux because they generally make less use of the technologies (e.g., flue gas scrubbers for power plants) and the fuels (e.g., natural gas) that yield lower soot. Soot is also implicated as a major cause of lung disease and other environmental harms, so most societies are likely to regulate soot more tightly over time and to welcome the opportunity to combine efforts to protect the climate with policies that deliver immediate local benefits that will make it easier to build a political coalition in favor of action. The atmospheric lifetime of soot is very short compared to the century-long lifetime of CO_2, and thus efforts to cut soot are not simple substitutes for mitigation of CO_2.

rapidly in the late 1990s, so did our emissions, making the Kyoto targets increasingly beyond the American grasp. By setting obligations in terms of the total volume of emissions, Kyoto unwittingly appeared to put environmental protection into direct conflict with economic growth. Indeed, when measured in terms of emission volumes the advanced industrialized countries that have performed best have done so through economic weakness. Germany shut down factories in the former East Germany; Luxembourg, which achieved the deepest percentage cut in emission volumes of any industrialized nation in the 1990s, owes its success to closing a major steel plant and relying more heavily on imported (rather than domestically generated) electricity.

When President Bush announced his climate change policy in February 2002, therefore, he adopted the measure of "greenhouse gas intensity"—the ratio of emissions to the size of the economy. He set a goal of cutting intensity by 18 percent over a decade. Figure 1 shows this measure for some key countries and reveals that the United States is in the pack. Our carbon intensity is about 210 grams of carbon emitted per dollar of economic output (gC/$). Japan and France rest at about two-thirds that value, reflecting aggressive energy-efficiency policies and high energy prices as well as large sources of carbon-free nuclear power in both countries' energy systems. By this measure, many developing countries actually appear worse than the United States. China's official statistics suggest a carbon intensity of around 300 gC/$. South Africa has among the highest carbon intensities (400 gC/$), as its heavy mining and industrial economy is based on the least costly electricity in the world, nearly all of it generated with carbon-intensive coal. India's carbon intensity is about the same as that of the United States, but the level is rising due to industrialization of the Indian economy.

So far, the United States is the only major country to focus on intensity as the measure of responsibility and progress. Two factors explain why others have not followed suit. First, President Bush's 18 percent target is widely seen as lacking ambition. The U.S. intensity peaked in 1922 and has been declining at about 18 percent per decade ever since (see Figure 1). Second, intensity is a

Carbon Intensity of Major Economies

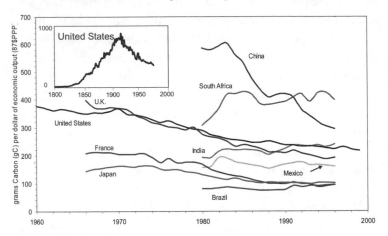

Figure 1: The Carbon Intensity of Major Industrialized and Developing Economies (in grams of carbon emitted as CO_2 per dollar of economic output). Inset shows carbon intensity for the United States from 1800.

Source: Oak Ridge National Laboratory (emissions statistics); U.S. Department of Commerce and the World Bank (economic output).

Notes: Economic output figures are converted into common dollar units using the World Bank's "purchasing power parities," which account for the higher local purchasing power of money in most developing countries. Use of market exchange rates would give developing countries much higher carbon intensities than the United States and other industrial economies. These data show only CO_2 emissions from burning fossil fuels and thus do not account for potentially important but less well-documented sources of greenhouse gases, such as CO_2 and methane released from the decaying biomass submerged in lakes behind hydroelectric dams. The data here also exclude deforestation (a major factor in the United States and other industrializing countries in the decades surrounding 1900 and a major factor today in Brazil and many forest-rich tropical nations) and emissions of methane from animal husbandry, the growing of certain crops (e.g., rice), drilling for oil and gas, and other sources.

convenient measure only in countries where the energy system is changing slowly and in favorable ways. In some countries, intensity measures are actually more volatile than total emissions, especially when the economy (the denominator in the intensity measure) changes abruptly. When the Soviet Union collapsed, for example, intensity rose sharply because the officially measured economy shrank more than total consumption of energy. Nor will all countries accept the premise that carbon intensity should decline over time. Brazil, for example, has traditionally relied on hydroelectric power and has therefore had an extremely low and stable carbon intensity (about 80 gC/$); now that most hydroelectric sites are already being used and Brazil has experienced costly blackouts during dry years, the government is encouraging construction of new fossil fuel–powered plants. Although a new pipeline from Bolivia, as well as recent gas finds in the ocean off of Rio de Janiero, has made it possible to use ultra-clean gas in these new plants, Brazil's carbon intensity is nonetheless set to rise. After long reliance on home-brewed liquid fuels made from sugar, oil-based products are also figuring more prominently in Brazil's energy system, and that too will raise carbon intensity.

Many developing countries favor per capita measures of accountability, which make them look responsible, as their populations are large relative to their emissions. China's per capita emissions are only one-tenth those of the United States. Some academics and a few diplomats from developing countries also favor an approach that would hold each nation accountable not only for its current emissions but also for the accumulated concentrations still lingering in the atmosphere from their past emissions. That historical approach would assign responsibility for about one-third of today's climate change to the United States, while developing countries (whose emissions have risen only recently) would account for only a small share. Such proposals appear harmful to U.S. interests because they imply that we have already spent a larger share of our part of the atmospheric budget. As you explore ways to engage other countries, however, you should be aware that they may measure responsibilities in ways that differ sharply from the metrics that the U.S. government finds most attractive.

INVESTING IN NEW TECHNOLOGIES

To the extent that you think climate change is a problem that merits limiting future emissions, you will need to consider the special role of technology policy. Adopting a credible limit on total emissions will send a strong signal to innovators. However, the technologies that will be needed probably will not arrive autonomously. Some will be prohibitively risky or expensive for private firms to develop solely on their own. It will be difficult for investors to appropriate all the benefits of their innovations, which is an additional reason why public programs will be needed to offset under-investment by the private sector.

To give you a sense of the magnitude of the technological task, consider that the entire world's economy today is powered with about 14 trillion watts (terawatts, or TW) of primary energy. Of that, about one-quarter emits essentially no greenhouse gases—mainly nuclear power and hydroelectricity, but also much smaller quantities of wind power and tiny amounts of solar power. Over the next fifty years, total world energy consumption may rise to about 35 TW. If the world decides to stabilize atmospheric concentrations of CO_2 over the next century at 550 ppm (about twice the pre-industrial level), then during the next fifty years the amount of carbon-free power must rise nearly fivefold. In other words, by 2050 the total amount of zero-carbon power supply must exceed the total power supply of all forms on Earth today. Historically, the supply of carbon-free energy has grown at only about 0.3 percent per year faster than the total energy supply. At that historical rate of "decarbonization," perhaps only 10 TW of carbon-free power will be available in 2050—an amount that is short by half of what would be needed to put the world economy on a path to stabilize the atmosphere. This calculation is merely an illustration, as nobody knows the true safe level for stabilizing concentrations. The value of 550 ppm is the one adopted by the European Union for planning purposes since 1996, and some firms (such as BP) have also loosely adopted such goals.[3]

There are many options available, from advanced nuclear plants to new wind turbines and perhaps exotic energy forms such as satel-

---

[3]If the arbitrary 550 ppm goal reflects the allowable climate forcing from all greenhouse gases (not just CO_2), then the allowable limit for CO_2 may be about one-fifth lower—roughly 450–500 ppm, depending on the assumptions for the emissions and concentrations of methane and other important greenhouse gases.

lites tethered in space that beam power collected from the sun back to Earth. None of these technologies, however, is ready to deploy in the large quantities needed. As you consider whether and how the federal government could play a role, you should be aware that there is a long and checkered history of U.S. policy intervention in the invention and deployment of new technologies. That history suggests four lessons that can guide your thinking.

First, there are many examples of technological spin-offs from government programs. Fuel cells, which convert hydrogen fuel into emission-free electricity and could become the backbone of a zero-carbon "hydrogen economy," are the by-product of academic tinkering in the nineteenth century applied in the space program. Transistors, the Internet, and many other technologies embedded in today's economy and society are also accidental offshoots of government programs and private tinkering that originally were directed at other goals. Who would have thought in the 1960s, when the Defense Department supported packet switching partly with the goal of creating a communications system that could withstand the disruption of nuclear war, that the Internet would result? These spin-offs are often used to justify open-ended technology programs in the belief that something useful will appear from the investment. That faith-based approach to technology policy could be wasteful because it is hard to predict which programs will be most effective.

Second, the desire for grand solutions to grand problems will yield political pressures for grand projects—a new "Manhattan Project" or "Apollo Program" to eliminate carbon. Such analogies are probably misplaced. Neither the construction of the first nuclear weapon nor putting a man on the moon required much attention to cost, and both were implemented within hierarchical military-style organizations. In contrast, completely transforming the economy will require enormous sensitivity to the cost and ease of transition—especially if many developing countries are to be enticed down low-carbon pathways. And the transition will occur within a market that operates most efficiently without hierarchical regulatory instructions.

The record of grand energy technology programs is generally not encouraging. Even programs that have succeeded in creating new technologies have often failed the test of markets. The U.S. Navy's nuclear submarine program provided most of the seed funding for light-water reactors; that support and the regulated utilities that bought most reactors explain why nuclear power rapidly diffused into widespread use in the U.S. electric power system. But those same protections also sheltered nuclear technology for too long from commercial considerations. Even more than the 1979 accident at Three Mile Island, the exorbitant and growing cost of reactors killed the industry. The potential for commercial improvement is evident in today's more competitive electric power market, in which new owners of reactors have found many innovative ways to squeeze about one-fifth more electricity from their plants than was typical in the old, highly regulated electricity system. Perhaps the worst failures in energy technology programs were the multi-billion-dollar efforts inspired by the oil crises of 1973 and 1979. A massive clean coal technology program, designed to make greater use of U.S. coal resources, was laden with special interests; politics, rather than market potential, drove the choice of technologies. In most large technology programs, such political distortions tend to arise as the programs become more visible and costly. It is hard to square the economic imperative for widgets in every congressional district with the need for nimble, efficient, and ruthless technology choices. In this thicket of troubles some success stories have nonetheless emerged. For example, a small program supported by the Department of Energy to develop high-efficiency electronic ballasts for fluorescent lights has accelerated the diffusion of this technology and saved hundreds of millions of dollars' worth of electricity.

The standard lesson from these programs is to avoid prematurely selecting "winners." It is difficult to put that advice into practice, however, and you should be wary of policy proposals that claim they will not anoint the early sprinters or political ponies. Managers of these programs find it relatively easy to avoid picking winners at the earliest basic research stages because supporting a diverse portfolio of fledgling ideas is relatively inexpensive. The real problem arises when technologies become sufficiently mature that a demonstration project is necessary. Almost always, industrial-scale demonstration of energy systems is very costly, and thus it is impossible to afford a large portfolio of projects. Today's conventional solution to this problem is to require reviews by outside experts, which can help avoid squandering resources on certain failures but often are unable to exert the subtle scrutiny that is needed throughout the management of successful projects.

Another standard remedy to this problem is to require private-sector co-financing. The private sector, it is thought, is unlikely to risk its money on poor commercial prospects; thus partnership with the private sector, in principle, can help select the most promising technologies. The Partnership for a New Generation of Vehicles (PNGV), a program adopted in the 1990s with the goal of enticing each U.S.-based auto manufacturer into producing an eighty-mpg prototype car, took this approach to sharing costs and following industry leadership (with outside expert review) in selecting technology pathways. The result was that PNGV followed paths that industrial partners probably would have followed on their own anyway—with PNGV, however, the research was, in effect, subsidized. And the attempt to distinguish between pre-commercial (public) research and commercial (private) research meant that useful findings were immediately appropriated by the private firms. As in pharmaceuticals, the rapid private appropriation of federally supported innovations has sped their appearance in the marketplace. Yet it may prove difficult to sustain public support for private appropriation especially if the commercial benefits of new products are highly visible.

In some respects, the PNGV program is deeply troubling. The eighty-mpg target bore little relation to realistic efficiency goals. While U.S. manufacturers toiled within PNGV, the Japanese manufacturers Honda and Toyota created hybrid cars that use ultra-efficient gasoline and electric motors in tandem. These cars achieve around fifty mpg today—nearly twice the level of conventional sedans—with the useful attribute that real people can afford to purchase them, and real people can actually drive them on real roads. In other respects, PNGV appears to have played a constructive role. It helped accelerate the diffusion from the national laboratories into application of new technologies and materials, such as a fuel cell designed at Los Alamos that required lower quantities of costly platinum.

Some technology partnership programs appear to have functioned well. The U.S. government created Sematech, a partnership with U.S. (and eventually international) semiconductor manufacturers that has proved profitable, has promoted common industry standards, and probably slowed the decline of U.S.-based semiconductor fabrication. (At the time, halting that loss was seen as a strategic goal for the economy and national security, which made Congress willing to appropriate the necessary funds.) The enterprise with the strongest record is the Defense Department's Advanced Research Projects Agency (DARPA), which deploys a large fund across a portfolio of innovative but risky projects. Like a venture capitalist, DARPA expects that only a few of its seeds will actually deliver blockbuster benefits, but the ones that do work pay for the entire portfolio. DARPA has thrived because of its connection to the defense agenda and the fact that most of its innovations have not required tests of commercial viability. If you adopt a technology policy that implies large amounts of spending on particular technologies—"winners"—you should consider the DARPA model rather than the moonshot or the Manhattan Project.

Third, it is very difficult to draw boundaries around the field of "energy" or "climate" technology. No field of scientific and technological research dominates the supply of plausible ideas for climate-neutral energy systems; new concepts can be found in high-energy physics, most fields of engineering, and chemistry. Biology is even a contender, as genetically engineered microbes could be jiggered to produce hydrogen. The hot field of nanotechnology also holds promise: microscopic carbon tubes, for example, could prove to be effective hydrogen storage devices. As it is impossible to identify the best frontier at the outset, it might be best to pursue a broad sprinkling of resources earmarked only loosely for topics such as "carbon-free energy" and "ultra-efficient energy systems" through existing basic science institutions—at the National Science Foundation, the Department of Energy, and (to a lesser degree) the National Institutes of Health. There is no good record of what the United States and other countries spend on such basic energy research, but the large probable return from a well-designed portfolio suggests that society (whether the United States or the world) probably dramatically underinvests in this area.

Fourth, radical and novel technologies are, to some extent, global public goods. International coordination of R&D may be needed. Whereas international coordination on controlling emissions of greenhouse gases is difficult because a large number of countries with highly disparate interests must be engaged, coordination on an international technology agenda is probably much easier. The United States, Japan, and the core group of large European nations together account for about 85 percent of world spending on R&D. All these nations already share a common (though not identical) interest in addressing the problem of climate change, and all have well-developed public institutions for administering sophisticated and costly research programs. There is a long history of collaboration among these nations on basic research programs, from joint experiments in the atmosphere to multi-billion-dollar scientific facilities, such as the European Organization for Nuclear Research (CERN), a high-energy physics facility on the French/Swiss border, and ITER, one of the next-generation facilities that will aim to demonstrate scientifically and economically viable nuclear fusion.

The more aggressive your technology policy on climate change, the greater will be the need for international collaboration. At present, there is almost no international collaboration on energy R&D, except in a few special areas marked by extremely expensive facilities (such as ITER) or a long history of international coordination (such as advanced fission nuclear reactors). The main international program in this area is managed by the International Energy Agency and consists of little more than governments declaring their own greenhouse gas R&D programs and exchanging broad reports with an international secretariat. Rarely do international collaborations lead to collective funding, but even efforts to achieve a coordinated research strategy could be beneficial.

The need for international coordination may be especially great for reasons that will be difficult for you to acknowledge publicly. Some technologies are so risky or stigmatized that they cannot be developed in the advanced industrialized world. In crop engineering, for example, Europe has slipped far behind the world's top innovators because of public concern about the technology. China appears to have reached the number two spot (just behind the United States) in crop genetic engineering due to a combination of generous government support for R&D, some pilfering of Western intellectual property, and, notably, lack of public opposition. Leadership in genetic engineering may determine the countries that lead the future of biological engineering for energy systems. In nuclear power, even the industrialized countries that have historically embraced that technology—Japan and France—find it ever harder to deploy new reactors. These difficulties have created niches for others. One of the promising new reactor designs is currently on the drawing boards at the South African electric power utility Eskom. Russia could also become a leader in the design and testing of new reactors.

The United States has already developed a technology strategy that incorporates some of these four lessons. The Climate Change Technology Program gives particular attention to two major projects. One involves co-funding (with industry) the FutureGen power plant—a potentially innovative project that would gasify coal and produce electricity while sequestering the resultant CO_2 underground. This plan builds on a long history of experiences with integrated gasification combined cycle (IGCC) power plants. Not only is this a promising way to decouple electricity production from the emission of CO_2 while allowing us to continue burning America's enormous coal reserves, but IGCC could also create a U.S.-based export market. IGCC plants are much more efficient than standard pulverized coal plants, and other nations will seek this technology as they face constraints on carbon while also wanting to make efficient use of their locally available coal resources. The other major element of U.S. technology investment is in hydrogen—notably the FreedomCAR initiative, a joint venture with U.S. automobile manufacturers to produce hydrogen-powered fuel cell cars as part of a shift to a hydrogen energy system. For these and other initiatives, including tax incentives for adoption of new technologies, the fiscal year 2005 budget request includes nearly $4 billion.

Although both these initiatives are admirable, earlier technology programs offer some warning lessons. In particular, we highlight the danger of pushing advanced technologies without any credible signal in the marketplace to favor investment in low-carbon systems. We also note that the FreedomCAR initiative is strikingly similar to some of the most flawed aspects of the PNGV venture, both in its parochial attention to U.S.-based auto manufacturers and in its embrace of the possibly irrelevant distant goal of a fuel cell–based hydrogen economy. The National Academy of Sciences recently reviewed the prospects for a hydrogen economy and concluded that the barriers such as onboard fuel storage in passenger cars remain formidable and the vision of a hydrogen economy—especially one centered on fuel cell–powered passenger vehicles—is probably more distant than is widely believed.

Finally, we note that your choices about technology policy for climate change are not isolated from other energy-related policies. These include subsidies, such as the many large subsidies that have been given to fossil fuels over the years, as well as the significant 1.8 cents per kilowatt hour (adjusted for inflation) production tax credit for wind power, which partly explains the rapid rise in this source of electric energy. (That subsidy expired at the end of 2003 but is likely to be renewed. For now, the lack of that subsidy cut the 2004 forecast for installation of new wind turbines from 2,000 megawatts to just 500 megawatts.) Wind power emits no CO_2, and wind power costs have declined markedly with greater experience building and operating wind turbines. Several states are experimenting with new power dispatch systems that can accommodate more easily the intermittent nature of wind power supplies. Many states have also adopted mandates to require certain fractions of the power supply from zero-carbon renewable fuels such as wind. Some have also created vibrant markets for tradable renewable power credits. Insofar as such policies encourage widespread application of low- and zero-carbon technologies, the need for additional active CO_2 limitations will diminish.

Another subsidy that has altered the landscape of the energy system is the Price-Anderson Act, which limits liability for nuclear power plant operators in case of accident and is widely seen in the industry as a prerequisite for construction of any new reactors. A new generation of more market-savvy nuclear reactors is on the drawing boards, and a comprehensive study by the Massachusetts Institute of Technology has shown that constraints on CO_2 could make these reactors competitive in U.S. electricity markets.

Perhaps the most important interaction between the carbon challenge and broader energy policy is the crisis in U.S. natural gas markets. Throughout the 1990s U.S. gas prices hovered around $2 per million British thermal units (BTU), but since 2000 they have climbed much higher (with peaks in spot markets above $20) as efforts to find new gas supplies in the continental United States are faltering and the main fields in Canada that supplied most of the incremental U.S. demand in the 1990s are being depleted. Most analysts expect that this shortfall will increasingly be filled by liquefied natural gas (LNG) from countries such as Trinidad, Nigeria, Qatar, Algeria, Australia, Indonesia, Russia, and Venezuela. Today, LNG accounts for just 1.5 percent of total U.S. gas supply, but that fraction may rise to perhaps to 10 percent over the next one to two decades. As LNG shares rise, U.S. gas prices will probably fall from their current high levels, but U.S. gas markets may become increasingly sensitive to events overseas as prices in U.S. markets are buffeted by competition in a world gas market that in many ways will be similar to the world market for oil.

The shift to gas, when it displaces coal, is good news for carbon intensity, since gas-fired power plants emit less than half the carbon per kilowatt-hour of electricity produced by standard coal plants. In the last decade there has been a strong preference for gas because those plants are less costly to build and have lower emissions of other environmental pollutants. Of all the new electric power capacity commissioned in 2003, 98.7 percent was fired by gas. High gas prices are forcing many of those plants to operate well below capacity. Builders of new plants are reconsidering their choice of fuels, and in the last year regulators have noted a sharp rise in the number of coal-fired plants that they have been asked to consider for approval. High gas prices have also encouraged electricity companies to form two new consortia to explore possible construction of new nuclear reactors.

Finally, the failure to adopt a comprehensive energy bill in 2004 left unsettled other issues that will affect the industry's ability to respond to the carbon challenge. Spending by the electricity industry on R&D appears to have been in a long slide; at present, electric utilities and generators invest barely 0.3 percent of their turnover in research. (Of major industries, only building materials and the railroads spend less of their turnover on research.) It is hard to reconcile the magnitude of the technological tasks facing the electricity industry with this very low level of R&D spending.

Potentially very important is the repeal of the Depression-era Public Utilities Holding Company Act (PUHCA), which has prevented most electricity companies from owning other utilities outside their home market. Absent PUHCA, the electricity industry probably would become financially much stronger, which should make it easier to encourage firms to take technological risks, especially if they see credible mandatory limits on their greenhouse gas emissions on the horizon. But the transition to a post-PUHCA era will be highly disruptive, with most firms focused on immediate survival and consumption of their rivals—an eat-or-be-eaten corporate ecology.

ENGAGING DEVELOPING COUNTRIES

If you are persuaded that efforts are needed to control emissions of greenhouse gases, then you must also decide whether and how to engage with developing countries. Politically and economically it will be difficult to avoid crafting a credible policy toward developing countries. For the last decade, developing country participation has been a litmus test for U.S. foreign policy on climate change. When large energy firms and their customers wanted to fan opposition to the Kyoto Protocol they ran advertisements in which the camera focused on a pair of scissors that cut around all the developing countries: exempting most of the world while regulating the United States and other industrialized nations, the voiceover proclaimed, was unfair and ineffective.

The demand for meaningful participation of developing countries was the centerpiece of the resolution sponsored in July 1997 by Senator Robert Byrd (D-WV) and Senator Chuck Hagel (R-NE). Intended to demonstrate U.S. resolve in advance of the final negotiations on the Kyoto Protocol that December, the resolution passed 95-0 and proclaimed that the Senate would not accept any treaty that did not also require that developing countries adopt "specific scheduled commitments ... within the same compliance period." That resolution cast a shadow over Kyoto, which did not impose any obligation on developing countries, and it has become a Rorschach test. Those who oppose limits on emissions point to the tersely worded resolution itself, which demands of developing countries what they adamantly refuse to accept. Those who advocate taking at least modest steps to limit U.S. emissions—including Senator Byrd himself—point to the floor debate that expressed the "sense of the Senate." Some senators in that debate interpreted the resolution as requiring identical and strict commitments for developing countries, while the interpretations of other senators were more liberal and elastic. As this resolution has attracted considerable public attention in the United States and overseas, we reproduce the resolution and excerpts from the floor debate in Appendix A.

Our deliberations have focused on four broad options for engaging developing countries. First, you could do nothing. This approach makes sense if you do not think that the climate problem merits much attention, or if you think that efforts to engage developing countries will end in failure. The "do-nothing" policy implies that the bulk of your climate policy will involve adaptation to the likely effects of climate change as well as low-cost and "no regrets" emission controls here in the United States.

Developing countries favor lack of engagement. They have expressed concern about climate change, and mounting evidence shows that they are more vulnerable than industrialized nations to storm surges, heat waves, drought, and other effects of a changing climate. Compared with advanced industrialized nations, their economies depend more on weather-related activities such as agriculture; they are less able to devote the capital to invest in climate-proofing for infrastructures; and they are less likely to build institutions such as systems for forecasting extreme weather events that can help reduce climate vulnerabilities. Their preference for inaction reflects not lack of concern and exposure but, rather, the higher priority they place on the immediate task of development. These countries know that the United States and other advanced industrialized countries developed without limitations on the use of fossil fuels. They also insist that advanced industrialized nations take the first steps in implementing meaningful policies before they themselves act; a grand compromise to that effect was codified in the United Nations Framework Convention on Climate Change. Many diplomats from developing countries argue that the industrialized nations—in particular, the United States—have broken that pledge, and thus efforts to engage developing countries have been additionally hampered by erosion of trust and credibility. It may prove relatively easy to reverse that erosion in the future by proffering substantial and concrete new proposals and incentives. For now, however, opposition to binding commitments is the one issue on which nearly all developing countries agree.

In the future it may be additionally difficult to gain these countries' participation since the Kyoto experience may be viewed increasingly as a false promise. The Clean Development Mechanism had been touted as a device for attracting foreign investment for projects that reduce emissions, but so far only three minor projects have gained approval. The World Bank has helped to jump-start the CDM by organizing the Prototype Carbon Fund (PCF)—a $180 million consortium of six governments (excluding the United States) and seventeen firms (none based in the United States) to fund a portfolio of CDM-like projects. Because the PCF's mandate is to promote only the highest quality projects, most of the PCF projects are sited in countries with strong domestic institutions. None is in the largest developing countries—such as China, India, Indonesia, and Malaysia. Just one project is in Brazil and one in South Africa. More than one-third of the PCF projects are in eastern Europe and do not involve developing countries at all. From the perspective of most of the key developing countries, the promised investments for climate protection are still elusive.

A second option is to demand that developing countries accept caps on their emissions. This approach requires sailing into strong diplomatic headwinds, and failure is likely. You could construct targets based on emission intensities or other metrics that developing countries find acceptable. As noted in Figure 1, Chinese emission intensity has declined sharply from about 600 gC/$ in the mid-1980s to around 300 gC/$ today. China is proud of that accomplishment, although perhaps half of the reduction reflects reported declines in the consumption of coal in China that many analysts believe are fictitious. It might be possible to design emission caps that reflect the interests of key developing countries and set with enough "headroom" to allow them to grow. You should be aware, however, that developing countries will refuse caps unless they are generous, but generous caps could undermine the integrity of emission trading systems in the United States and other industrialized countries. Generous caps could be akin to the vast windfall of surplus emission credits awarded to Russia in Kyoto; failure to enforce trading rules within developing countries could lead to a flood of bogus emission permits from those nations into permit trading systems elsewhere in the world.

It might be possible to force developing countries to accept strict caps by linking this issue to other matters, perhaps within the World Trade Organization. Such linkages will be difficult to craft and will probably backfire. The WTO agenda is already overcrowded, and developing countries (as well as most trade experts) are already opposed to integrating an ever-expanding list of environmental standards into trade rules. The effects of loading environmental, labor, human rights, and other standards on the world trading system may include the loss of well-being for all nations by raising barriers to trade as well as increasing the risk that new trade rounds will fail to make progress due to conflicts over these new rules and standards. By undermining economic development, such countries could make developing countries more vulnerable to climate change than otherwise would be the case.

You might try to reduce opposition in the developing world to accepting limits on emissions by raising awareness in these nations of the dangers of climate change. In the past, the U.S. government has provided some support to research programs and civic groups in developing countries with this aim. Such campaigns are difficult to organize, however, and unlikely to have any substantial near-term effects. The standard response from developing country diplomats—demanding that the United States, especially, take the lead in controlling emissions—will be difficult to counter. Insofar as there is any awareness of climate dangers in developing countries, it is usually organized by NGOs that are nearly uniform in their view that the industrialized countries (in particular the United States) are the root cause of this problem. Calling attention to climate change may raise the visibility of that argument, which could actually make it harder to achieve meaningful action in developing countries.

A third approach involves reinvigorating the Kyoto system, in particular the CDM. In our review of the efforts to elaborate the Kyoto system we found the CDM system to be encumbered with complicated rules and highly politicized procedures. However, these problems may have remedies. Procedures for approving CDM projects could be streamlined; true experts rather than politically instructed diplomats could be empowered to make more of the key decisions about the level of credit that would be awarded for projects. Additionally, you could put pressure on the members of the Kyoto Protocol to abandon the practice of shunning certain types of projects, such as nuclear plants and large hydroelectric dams, from receiving CDM credit. Another critical piece of reform for the CDM would be to insist that a new and improved CDM allow credits for tropical forest conservation and management projects. The U.S. government has consistently supported projects to preserve nature, and at the same time such projects can help avoid emissions of carbon that would come from deforestation and other changes in natural landscapes. However, many types of these projects have been excluded from receiving due credit under the CDM before 2012 (and perhaps thereafter as well). You could build a coalition for forestry reform in the CDM by allying with Brazil, Indonesia, and several other forest-rich nations that are themselves trying to attract more resources for forest protection. If the United States were to reengage with the Kyoto process it could make such reforms of the CDM a condition of its return. If the United States were to stay outside the Kyoto process but establish its own national emission trading system, it could create a scheme that operates in parallel with the CDM but with more efficient and sensible rules. Credits would then flow through the U.S. system instead of the CDM. Since the United States would be such a large market, the United States could, in effect, impose a superior alternative.

Many other countries would welcome a strategy that reinvigorates the CDM. A more effective CDM would be useful not only for developing countries that host investments but also for the main industrialized nations. A recent report from the European Environment Agency suggests that the European Union will miss its Kyoto target by a few percent, mainly because emissions from transportation are rising more rapidly than expected. European firms and governments may need to purchase emission credits overseas to make up the difference. Japan and Canada are also likely to fall short on their targets; they, too, will need outside credits. So long as the CDM remains hobbled and inefficient, the paper credits in Russia and Ukraine remain the only large quantities of credits available on international markets, giving these countries excessive influence and reducing the tangible benefits that developing countries obtain from sustaining their engagement with the Kyoto process.

There are substantial risks stemming from a strategy focused on reforming the CDM, however. Leveraging changes in the CDM by reengaging with the Kyoto Protocol will require making promises that might be hard to fulfill. It proved impossible even for the Clinton administration, which professed deep concern about the climate change problem, to ready the Kyoto Protocol for Senate consent. Many of the CDM's deficiencies are already written into the Kyoto system—either into the Kyoto treaty itself (e.g., the discouragement of nuclear power projects) or into the procedures that govern the CDM, which were painstakingly negotiated over a four-year process that largely finished in 2001. With so much time and effort invested, many countries may be unwilling to revisit closed deals. Perhaps only a spectacular failure of the Kyoto Protocol will force the necessary rethinking. Moreover, many observers claim that it will be impossible to make the CDM system work efficiently even under the best conditions. These observers claim that it is impossible to make the hypothetical "baseline" calculation—the level of emissions that would result in the absence of a particular project. The experience to date suggests that these observers are probably correct, and that partly explains why the CDM has attracted much less investment than enthusiasts had originally hoped. A major push by the United States could yield sustainable reforms to the CDM, but even after such reinvigoration the patient may still be mortally wounded.

Fourth, you could craft a new strategy for engaging with developing countries. The three options presented so far—disengagement, emission caps, and an offset scheme such as the CDM—have dominated most policy discussion for the last decade. None has had much impact on the behavior of developing countries. The fourth strategy could involve working with developing countries to craft "climate-friendly" development strategies. Unlike the CDM, which aims to animate investment by awarding credits, this approach could attempt to put climate issues into the mainstream of development policy. It could focus on broad policy initiatives, such as investment in natural gas infrastructures that make it easier for countries to operate natural gas–fired electricity generators where they otherwise would build less efficient and more carbon-heavy coal-fired ones. Many countries are already making such investments. China and India, for example, are in the midst of installing large gas infrastructures. In China these include a pipeline from gas reserves in the western part of the nation to Beijing and Shanghai, as well as LNG terminals in southern coastal cities. In India these infrastructure projects include new gas pipelines, incentives to develop newly discovered offshore gas reserves, and India's first-ever operational LNG terminal, which took its first delivery in January 2004. At the same time, a program to develop advanced coal power plants that allow for sequestration of CO_2 could help developing countries that are rich in coal reserves (such as China, India, Indonesia, and South Africa) gain confidence that taking the climate problem seriously will not undermine their efforts to supply electricity and other modern energy services. (In crafting the FutureGen project the Bush administration sought to engage developing country partners. However, the outcome of those partnership discussions remains uncertain; if FutureGen is funded fully and yields successful innovations, minds will focus on protection and ownership of FutureGen's intellectual property, which could undermine efforts to engage foreign partners.) Within the CDM system such broad programs to create the physical and intellectual infrastructure for low-carbon futures would never gain any credit because it would be too difficult to quantify the long-term and highly leveraged effects of these investments across the entire economy.

For the United States, this strategy of mainstreaming climate into development would require working principally with the major policy organs in developing countries that are responsible for development—for example, finance, industry, and planning ministries. The U.S. role could involve supporting activities that would help countries realize their own development goals in ways that also incidentally reduced carbon emissions. The advantage of this approach is that it would involve swimming with the tide— identifying activities that the host government would favor (and fund) already and activities that already align with the interests of private profit-making ventures. For example, the United States already has extensive development assistance programs in major developing countries, mainly through the U.S. Agency for International Development (USAID). These programs include attention to the improvement of energy efficiency and to reorganization of energy systems in ways that encourage investment in modern technologies. A slight refocus of these programs could make carbon a central organizing principle; by helping these countries reorganize their energy systems to make them more profitable and to serve better the needs of the local population, such programs could also lower the intensity of greenhouse gas emissions. Among the successes, USAID programs have already helped countries identify ways to make fuller use of low-carbon renewable power. For example, in India a USAID project has helped a sugar cane refinery recycle crop wastes to generate heat and electricity, which has reduced the need for fossil fuel energy.

This development-linked approach could leverage large amounts of emission reductions. However, it also carries many dangers. Developing countries may simply choose to embrace those programs that they would pursue anyway. By design, the exact reduction in emissions will be difficult to quantify, which will lead many environmental groups to claim that the "mainstreaming" approach is simply a rhetorical device that only pretends to deliver real solutions to the climate problem. The program could create expectations that it will become a large source of funds that, inevitably, will yield disappointment. The West-East pipeline in China, for example, involves $20 billion in mainly Chinese investment. In such huge projects it may be difficult for relatively tiny amounts of climate change–related programmatic funding to have much effect. If the World Bank had participated in China's Three Gorges hydroelectric dam, for example, it would have leveraged its funding by demanding the application of Western environmental and human rights standards. Wary, the Chinese government raised the needed capital on its own—outside the bank's purview.

INFORMING THE PUBLIC

The sixth major dimension in which you face policy choices is communication with the public. Public opinion about climate change is highly malleable. Awareness of climate change is high, but willingness to act has varied considerably, and understanding of the underlying processes and options is poor.

A survey of polls by the Program on International Policy Attitudes (PIPA) at the University of Maryland found that a small minority of the U.S. population dismisses the theory of climate change altogether. A Gallup poll in March 2001 revealed that slightly more than half of Americans thought that the majority of scientists believe that global warming is occurring. Americans generally know very little about Kyoto. A Pew poll in April 2001—in the middle of the firestorm about the Bush administration's withdrawal from Kyoto—found that only 26 percent of those polled were willing to venture an opinion as to whether we had withdrawn from the treaty. Interestingly, some evidence suggests that public support for Kyoto has risen since 2001 even as it has become increasingly implausible that the United States could ever meet its Kyoto commitments.

Willingness to pay for emission controls varies especially with the state of the economy. In 2000, when the public perceived the economy as strong, a Gallup poll showed a majority willing to support environmental goals even at the expense of the economy. Two years later, as the economy faltered, that public commitment had dropped considerably. A January 2002 poll by ABC News and the *Washington Post* ranked environmental issues far down the list of priorities—below the campaign against terrorism, economic growth, education, Social Security, health care, national defense, prescription drugs for the elderly, and balancing the federal budget. A PIPA poll in October 1998 suggested that two-thirds of Americans were willing to spend $50 per household (or less) to comply with the Kyoto Protocol; that number is comparable to the estimated cost per household from a study done by President Bill Clinton's Council of Economic Advisers (CEA) on the cost of meeting Kyoto. The CEA study implied that about 85 percent of the effort at reducing emissions would take the form of overseas investments through Kyoto's international emission trading and CDM systems. Yet the PIPA poll showed that most Americans opposed emission trading until the concept was explained. Then, 65 percent favored trading with less developed countries. Yet the CEA's own analysis implied that most trading would probably occur with Russia—a scenario that the main pollsters have not explored.

Politically, the renewed attention to security in the wake of September 11, 2001, could affect the ease of building public support for action on climate change and the technological options available. Greater public attention to energy security could improve the prospects for policies that boost energy efficiency and renewable energy, which would lower the trajectory for U.S. emissions of CO_2. At the same time, however, concerns about terrorism could make it harder to site LNG facilities and nuclear power plants, which could push the U.S. electric power system back to greater reliance on coal and locally available renewable sources. If coal is the main winner then the U.S. emissions trajectory would rise—indeed, with natural gas pries at historically high levels investors in new power generation equipment are examining the option of building new coal plants. Concerns about energy security could be used to build a coalition for developing advanced coal gasification facilities that also sequester carbon—as in the FutureGen project that is already advancing. Security could become the glue that binds broad public support to a wide array of yet undetermined elements of energy policy. Similarly, concern about gasoline prices—which

[65]

rose sharply in 2004 due to shortages in refining capacity and high crude oil prices—could also fan public concern in a variety of malleable directions, including toward mandates for higher fuel efficiency.

Regardless of your policy we recommend that you devote considerable effort to explaining it to the public. If you choose a minimal course of action focused primarily on adaptation and developing innovative technologies—which we represent in the first speech—we think you should explain why the climate change problem does not require an urgent effort. In February 2002, when President Bush announced his administration's policy, he did not articulate a fundamental view of the climate issue; rather, President Bush raised concerns about the costs of action, which is a line of argument that his opponents may blunt easily by arguing that technologies are available to control emissions and that the threat of changing climate is so severe that it requires radical action. The case for minimal action would be easier for the public to understand if you demonstrate that the climate problem does not pose challenges that are substantially different from other environmental challenges. No American president has ever articulated these views, yet the public is inclined to believe that environmental quality is deteriorating—implying that environmental problems require drastic responses—even though many key measures of our environmental health have improved dramatically in recent decades.

If you choose to support reinvigorating the Kyoto system—the course represented in our second speech—then you will need to explain why the United States withdrew from Kyoto in the first place and why it makes sense to reengage. At present, the small fraction of the American public that pays attention to Kyoto-related matters probably also views the U.S. exit as evidence of arrogant American unilateralism. This second speech argues that the Bush administration had no choice because the United States never could have complied with the Kyoto targets—a point President Bush made in March 2001 when he withdrew from Kyoto, but the point was lost in the furor of the moment. You can acknowledge that the public has deep concerns about this issue but point out the inconsistency between public expectations of what it would cost to meet Kyoto's requirements and the likely reality. You can articulate how reengagement with Kyoto will yield enormous diplomatic leverage that the United States can use to make Kyoto more effective and less discriminatory—thus shaping the mental model of "Kyoto" away from a particular set of (unachievable) obligations into a process that needs American guidance.

Finally, if you choose to articulate a different pathway—as we outline in the third speech—then the public will need your vision as a guide. The third speech suggests that the problem of climate change requires a reduction in long-term emissions, but it argues that the best approach does not correspond with today's conventional wisdom. It argues for a decentralized bottom-up approach rather than a top-down treaty-based system as in Kyoto.

In almost every aspect of this issue—the natural science, the economics, the role of firms, public administration, etc.—the public is exposed to a wide range of conflicting opinions. The public needs help to frame the issues, to establish models and analogs, and to comprehend what is at stake, because all the major elements of the climate problem—its causes, effects, and remedies—are beyond the grasp of normal human experience.

SUMMARY OF THE THREE OPTIONS

We have organized the wide array of policy choices into three broad options. Each is a coherent package of choices drawn from the six dimensions articulated above. We underscore, however, that these three options are hardly the only possible combinations.

Adaptation and Innovation
This option rests on the notion that uncertainties in the science of climate change make spending substantial resources on the control of emissions premature. The speech underscores that some amount of climate change is inevitable as emissions continue to rise from

the industrialized and especially the developing nations; the effects of a changing climate, however, are unlikely to be different from variations in weather and climate that we already experience, and thus adaptation will be relatively easy. The speech also underscores that although analysts have identified many ways to control emissions at low cost, in practice these measures are likely to be much more difficult to implement; there is great risk, therefore, that the cost of controlling emissions will be high, possibly very high. This option thus presents the minimal effort that probably could be justified. It envisions voluntary programs to control emissions from the energy system and also through better protection of tropical forests. It advocates modest investment in new technologies that might yield breakthroughs as well as continued investment in science so that we can improve understanding of the problem and gain early warning of approaching dangers.

Advantages
- Minimal budgetary cost. While the economy is recovering and federal budgets are tight, this option carries the minimal cost to industry and to the federal government.
- Emphasizes the normal adaptive capacity of the economy. Articulates a reason—adaptation—for why the United States should not impose draconian controls on emissions. This reason is probably more durable than simply arguing that the science is uncertain; the American public has proved that it is willing to spend large resources combating uncertain hazards, such as food contamination, asbestos, air pollution, nuclear war, and terrorism. The arguments about uncertain science have had credibility with a small (and probably shrinking) minority. Adaptation, if articulated clearly, has the potential to be more convincing.
- Domestic interests. This option focuses narrowly on U.S. interests; it does not attempt to appeal to wooly notions of international justice by speculating about the dangers of climate change in developing countries.

• Gives priority to industrial growth. This policy is unlikely to disrupt incumbent industries in the production and use of oil, gas, and coal. The investment in new technology might yield technologies that could aid U.S. business and create jobs in the future.

Disadvantages
• Adaptation is seen as non-action. The argument for minimal action is subtle and rests on our ability to adjust to changes in the environment. Opponents might characterize this response as "let them eat pollution." Americans have generally not tolerated policies that acknowledge the existence of an environmental problem while simultaneously claiming that the problem poses little danger. If adaptation is your policy it might be more effective not to give a high-profile speech calling attention to the issue.
• Public backlash. If the climate change problem becomes a major issue then public support for more aggressive action—controls on emissions—will grow stronger. The lack of any binding controls may make it hard for you to retain credibility in that context.
• Offensive to some allies. Other nations will view this as inadequate, especially as it is hostile to the Kyoto system. Good or not, Kyoto remains the dominant international institution by far on the subject of climate change.
• Potentially disadvantageous to U.S. business. Insofar as you believe that limits on carbon may be imposed eventually, a rousing speech against binding limits may actually harm U.S. industry by protecting it (temporarily) from the need to plan for a carbon-constrained future. U.S. firms may be less able to compete against firms that have already found ways to cut carbon, and U.S. exporters will not have developed the technologies needed to compete in the global market.

Reinvigorating Kyoto

This speech defines climate change as the most serious international environmental issue of our era. It argues that the effort to cut carbon should become an organizing principle for U.S. foreign policy, and it suggests that most of the solutions to the climate problem will improve America's energy security while also protecting the planet's ecosystems, on which all life depends. It envisions reengagement with the Kyoto process because creating an alternative to Kyoto would require a huge effort for little benefit. Serious solutions to the climate problem will require global engagement, and this speech argues that most other nations are already engaged productively in the Kyoto regime. This speech explains that the United States had no choice but to abandon Kyoto's unrealistic short-term targets; it demands renegotiation of the Kyoto targets and the setting of fair targets for developing countries. It argues that short-term targets should be set in the context of a long-term goal for stabilizing the atmosphere. Although nobody knows what concentration of greenhouse gases in the atmosphere is truly safe, this speech suggests starting with the goal of 550 ppm— twice the pre-industrial level. It demands reform of the CDM to make it more efficient and to allow credit for the protection of the world's diminishing tropical forests. The speech underscores that adaptation to the most worrisome effects of climate change is not possible, and it argues that it is unjust to impose a changing climate on developing countries that are already struggling to make ends meet.

Advantages
- Requires emission reductions. A large centrist group of voters probably favors some binding action to control emissions, though their exact willingness to pay for control is unknown.
- Appealing to core constituency for climate policy. It recognizes and supports the Kyoto system as the only existing international framework; it emphasizes the need to start now with the implementation of policies to bend emission trajectories.

- Olive branch to nations devoted to Kyoto. Other industrialized nations, especially Canada, Japan, and the members of the European Union, will see this as a reengagement with an institution (Kyoto) that is very important to them.
- Tough but fair with developing countries. This speech outlines a plan for engaging developing countries that is consistent with at least some interpretations of the Byrd-Hagel resolution.
- Concrete strategy. Offers a vision for addressing a problem that, at least periodically, commands public concern.

Disadvantages
- Presently not credible. You do not have the votes in either the House or the Senate to adopt the national policies that would be needed to make such a strategy credible. Getting the votes will require considerable presidential effort to shape public priorities and understanding of the issue. Other policy priorities will probably suffer. So long as the public is focused on the economy and the war on terrorism, concern about environmental issues (especially distant global issues) has remained low, and thus the electoral benefits from investing in this strategy may be small.
- Unknown cost. A well-designed policy can minimize cost, but opponents will portray this as a scheme to tax energy that could bankrupt the economy; those same opponents were effective in organizing opposition to the Kyoto commitments on similar grounds.
- Risk of diplomatic failure. Developing countries and other nations that are reluctant to control their emissions (e.g., Russia) will be furious, as they have adamantly opposed meaningful limits on their emissions. Reaching agreement with them could be extremely difficult unless you allow liberal "headroom" in their targets (which will recreate the problem of surplus credits with Russia under Kyoto). If you set strict targets for the United States, however, industry will demand strict targets for the rest of the world as well—the more headroom you supply to others the harder it will be to gain consent here in Amer-

ica. To brandish a stick at these reluctant nations you might need to link this issue to other matters of importance to developing countries such as trade talks, but that could complicate and undermine U.S. objectives in those other areas.

Making a Market

This speech also argues that the climate problem is a serious long-term threat to America's prosperity. However, it articulates a dramatically different approach. It sees the Kyoto framework as unworkable because it tries to create a global emission trading system from the "top down," whereas the most successful international regulatory regimes are built from the "bottom up." This speech gives little attention to the science and effects of climate change, except to declare that the evidence is strong enough to warrant prudent action. It focuses instead on changing the public understanding of the problem at hand, comparing the task of building a global trading system to the creation of a new form of money. It argues that we must focus on establishing integrity in that monetary system by working first with a small group of other countries—first and foremost the European Union—that have a common interest in creating a strong currency. The speech argues that we must move slowly and cautiously in that effort, as failure will undermine the value of the currency and erase the political will and public trust needed to sustain action.

The speech focuses on the need for action by the United States to establish its own emission trading system and, having designed the best procedures for the United States, to negotiate links to other trading systems. Such American unilateralism, it argues, is necessary to avoid mistakes of the past, such as the failure of the Kyoto rules to create incentives to encourage the protection of tropical forests. It argues that unilateralism is essential and that a global framework will be the by-product—not the cause—of meaningful action in key leading nations. In this system there will be multiple currencies that reflect different experimental efforts to establish the best rules and institutions; over time, those diverse national efforts will converge into a global scheme as the best rules and procedures supplant the worst.

At the same time, the U.S. government must work with leading innovative firms to make a market for new energy technologies, so that investments in advanced renewable power technologies, hydrogen energy systems, nuclear power, and other options can enter the niche markets where experience and competition will lead to improvement. Such markets do not arise spontaneously; over time, the best new technologies will make it possible to achieve the deep cuts in carbon that are needed to stabilize the climate.

Advantages
- Bold and direct. As with the second speech, you will probably gain political benefits by visibly addressing the seriousness of the climate change problem and by reengaging with an international process by offering a credible vision for a global strategy.
- Market based. This vision takes the market—and the history of market-making—as its centerpiece. It will resonate with business and it will allow you to build on the increasing use of market-based measures for protecting the environment, which have demonstrated a clear record of success. This will be attractive to centrist voters, including many Republicans.
- Unique and innovative. The speech can be memorable because it does not map easily on any of the options that are debated in the mainstream today. A sharp break with the failing past, rooted in a strong commitment to an effective solution, will force the pundits to think and debate. A by-product of all that would be continued free attention for your way of solving the problem.
- Possibility for international cooperation. Pursuing a different track within a multilateral vision offers a chance of diplomatic success. Frustration with Kyoto is leading some governments to search for alternative international arrangements, but so far the United States has not offered an attractive rival vision. At the same time, offering an explicit link to the Euro-

pean trading system will be attractive to key allies (notably the United Kingdom). The EU system is new and fragile; outside recognition will help to establish its legitimacy.

• Flexibility of unilateral action. By reserving a large role for unilateral choice you can tune the stringency and timing of the U.S. effort to the levels that you think will gain approval in Congress. You can build on the existing McCain-Lieberman proposal as a foundation for constructing a politically sustainable coalition in favor of a U.S. national trading system. The registries of emissions that several states, such as California, have developed can provide a foundation for setting baselines and determining the level of emission controls that is politically achievable. These leading states already have laid some of the groundwork needed to develop a political coalition for a carbon market.

Disadvantages
• Confirms rejection of Kyoto. The attack on Kyoto will produce negative reactions in many quarters, and that could complicate the task of building domestic support.

• Irritates developing countries. By arguing that the current approach to engagement with developing countries is not working you will force developing countries to confront the eventual need to undertake binding obligations. You may be able to blunt their opposition by using examples of current bilateral U.S. programs in developing countries as examples of investment and technology transfer that would expand with the creation of stronger market signals to invest in low-carbon energy systems. However, the credibility of such promises is low, and thus bringing the developing countries on board may require an explicit grand bargain with identifiable tangible outcomes. Crafting that could be very difficult and possibly expensive.

• Complex. Outlining a new vision on a complicated subject inevitably leads to a complicated speech. Communication may be easier if you adopt simple slogans and messages that correspond with what the public already thinks about the climate issue and its solution.

- Uncertain success. A grand alternative vision, announced with fanfare, is a liability if you do not see it through to realization.

RECOMMENDATION

We recommend that you convene a meeting of your key economic, science, and national security advisers, employing this memo and the three alternative speeches as a starting point for the discussions. We suggest that you develop a policy by giving feedback on the options addressed here, leading to one central choice that can serve as a platform for constructing your policy. With that platform we can then elaborate a fuller policy and speech that you would present to the nation and to our allies.

SPEECH ONE: ADAPTATION AND INNOVATION

LOCATION: Massachusetts State House, Boston

My Fellow Americans:

We gather today in the great city of Boston to discuss the issue of our changing climate—what some call "global warming." Every nation on Earth, including the United States, causes its share of climate change. Every nation will be affected, though some less than others.

How shall we confront this planetary problem? The answers to this question are not nearly as difficult as the newspapers, scare shows, and pseudo-documentaries would have you believe. Climate change is no greater than other challenges that we have faced and easily overcome.

Imagine, before we begin, the scene just one hundred years ago. A speaker in this august chamber who was asked to comment on the pressing environmental problem of that day would have given his address over to the matter of mud and dung. The streets were full of it, and when the rains came it flowed amply and everywhere. Travel was next to impossible.

Bostonians overcame the challenge. They paved the roads and built storm sewers. As they sought faster and more flexible means of transport they traded horses for cars, which also cut the noxious fumes.

We, too, will overcome the challenge by changing our environment and by embracing new technologies. As we contemplate crafting a strategy to address global warming—the effects of which will manifest themselves, if ever, over fifty to one hundred years—perhaps the biggest danger is that we become single-minded about this threat and let ourselves be blindsided by other problems and opportunities. Let us hope that the leader elected by our great-great-grandchildren does not chastise us for tunneling vast resources into clever and costly solutions to today's equivalent of the mud crisis, only to find that the real world had moved on. We can serve our descendants better by focusing on fundamentals— by investing in economic growth and knowledge that can be passed across the generations.

Today I would like to explain the real nature of the threat of climate change, what we are doing already, and how your federal government will pursue a balanced response in the coming months and years.

There is little doubt that the climate is, indeed, warming. Scientists around the globe—including at the nearby Massachusetts Institute of Technology—have painstakingly assembled records from weather stations, ship buoys, and sundry other sources. The record is pretty clear. Since the 1950s the global temperature has risen by half a degree. Many scientists think we are on a path to raise the average temperature another few degrees over the next century. Sea level will rise a bit, which will affect some places in the United States. But in other places, such as the Gulf of Alaska and much of the Canadian Pacific Northwest, sea level is actually falling as the continents rise slowly out of the oceans— they are still rebounding from the weight of the glaciers during the last ice age.

Beyond that, the scientific crystal ball gets cloudier. Even the simplest questions—such as whether Earth is warmer today than at any moment in recent millennia—have no simple answers. Some experts say that climate change will cause more frequent and intense storms. Others disagree. So far there is little firm evidence either way. Some claim that wet areas will get wetter, and areas prone to drought will get dryer. There seems to be some agreement that hot summers will get hotter in most places. But the likely effects of a changing climate include good things as well. Cold winters probably will become less intense in most places, and we must not forget that in much of the country the winter cold is a bigger killer than heat.

The uncertainty does not stop there. As my administration reviewed the evidence we also found that our best economists don't really

[77]

know the cost of controlling emissions of the so-called greenhouse gases that cause climate change. Most greenhouse gases are released when we burn fossil fuels and thus are an essential part of the modern economy. You may have heard about policies that can reduce emissions at zero cost. We looked at those policies as well, and it turns out that even these "free" policies are often laden with hidden costs and perverse effects.

We do know that voluntary efforts can reduce emissions without imposing much burden on the economy. For several years this nation has had a bipartisan policy allowing firms to register their voluntary efforts to lower their greenhouse gas emissions. The list of participants is long and distinguished.

Similarly, the government has sponsored a host of other programs that have helped businesses of all sizes, as well as American households, reduce their energy consumption through more efficient technologies. Next time you buy a TV or computer monitor, look for the decal with the rainbow and the star—the sign of your government's "Energy Star" program, which helps consumers identify products that sip energy while not compromising on functionality. These programs—voluntary incentives and information for smart consumers—are examples of government at its nimble best.

But alongside these successful programs is a minefield of failure—a long list of wrongheaded policies that past administrations have designed around the false idea that government knows best. These policies have tied firms and consumers in red tape; they have blocked innovation and stripped consumers of their power to choose. They undermine our competitiveness and threaten our way of life.

For example, my administration has opposed radical new efficiency standards that will be imposed on the manufacturers of new air conditioners. Quite often, higher efficiency is not free—it requires making a more expensive product that is not affordable for everyone. For households that survive paycheck to paycheck, these new standards would force them to spend even more of their scarce savings on something that they need. Is it right for government to assume that you, the consumer, are unable to read the labels on products and decide for yourself what is best?

And that is just the beginning. Some of the professional global warming pundits claim that protecting the climate requires cutting world emissions by half or more. Yet developing countries are adamantly opposed to doing anything about the threats of climate change. They say that they have other priorities—development, for one. These nations already account for half of the world's net emissions of greenhouse gases, and their emissions are rising rapidly. That means that a deep cut in global emissions will require America and the rest of the industrialized world to do more— much more than our share. In this global economy, how can we expect our factories to compete with those in China, Brazil, or India if we are hobbled by a costly mandate to eliminate fossil fuels from our economy while they face no such constraint?

I can appreciate why the developing countries are putting development first. They know that wealth will make them better able to adapt to environmental stresses, including climate change. Development is such an important, overriding goal that my administration has created a novel "Millennium Challenge Corporation" that will deliver development assistance to the countries that will make the best use of our help.

We should not lament development. It is our moral duty to help where we can, and a growing world economy is good news for us as well: it will breed fewer terrorists and offer bigger markets.

Some still say that it will be inexpensive—perhaps even profitable—to eliminate fossil fuels from our economy. They imagine that we will stumble on some miracle energy source that satisfies our need for energy services yet is free of carbon dioxide and causes no other types of harmful pollution. That's a tall order. Your government, along with industry, has redoubled its support for research and development on a portfolio of promising technologies. So far, however, nothing seems likely to deliver the magic bullet.

Serious strategies to combat global warming require abandoning old prejudices. We must, for example, take a fresh look at nuclear power. I find it encouraging that several utilities are likely to announce in the coming few years that they will commit funds to building the next generation of nuclear reactors. I know that many people are opposed to nuclear reactors, but we must look carefully at the risks and benefits. Nuclear power is one of the cleanest ways to make electricity. With the price of natural gas high, as it has been for the last two years, nuclear power is also economically competitive. Many of the obstacles to a rebirth of the nuclear power industry are being cleared. The Price-Anderson Act, which holds reactor owners accountable for their actions yet puts a reasonable cap on their liability, is up for renewal. Without this legislation, no sane company would invest in nuclear technology, which already supplies about one-fifth of the electricity that America needs while emitting no greenhouse gases.

We have finally opened the permanent repository for spent fuel at Yucca Mountain in Nevada. With the Federal Energy Regulatory Commission, we are making progress in introducing market forces to the U.S. electric power system. In the last decade alone, as market forces have come to the U.S. electric power system, new managers have dramatically improved the performance of U.S. reactors. Across the United States, the cost of wholesale electricity generated from nuclear plants has actually declined about two-fifths as market-sensitive operators have found ways to cut costs and keep their reactors online generating electricity for more hours every year.

We must also explore ways to make use of America's abundant coal reserves. Several major utilities, along with the federal government, have launched the FutureGen program to study and demonstrate a promising technology called coal gasification. This technology will make it possible to generate electricity and hydrogen fuels from our nation's abundant coal reserves while capturing the carbon dioxide and putting it safely underground. Like nuclear power, coal gasification will also help us improve our energy security by making the best use of resources we have at home.

We are making sound investments in these new technologies. But it is one thing to back novel technologies with uncertain delivery and quite another to bet our economic future by imposing strict limits on emissions. Until we know more about what it will really cost to control emissions it is not possible to justify imposing binding limits on emissions. The American economy has grown admirably when we have made full use of our capital base, including the flexible energy infrastructure that rests mainly on the power of fossil fuels. Government must focus on ways to multiply the productivity of capital, not erase it.

You elected me to spur economic growth in America. We are energizing the economy, and we won't threaten America's economic health with ill-conceived limits on fossil fuels aimed at achieving a highly uncertain impact on a highly uncertain problem that we probably can't control anyway.

My administration's thorough review of the climate change issue has also revealed that the likely effects of climate change are not as serious as some say. A few degrees' change in global average temperature is within the realm of what we already experience. As you know here in Boston, some months are warmer than average, and others are colder. Variation in rainfall will affect our reservoirs and farmers, but America's quiver of responses to a changing climate is stuffed full of effective arrows. When farmers see the real price of water rise they have found myriad ways to cut their consumption, such as through the deployment of new seed and crop varieties. In some settings they have also installed drip irrigation—itself an innovation from water-starved Israel, proving once again that necessity is the mother of invention. We can respond and adapt easily, if American ingenuity is allowed to work its magic.

In my meetings with civic leaders here in Boston I have heard fears that rising sea levels will swamp the city. But it is important to recognize that higher sea levels, if they occur at all, will manifest themselves over decades, during which time we can easily prepare for change. Again, it is important to put the long time scales that are relevant for global warming into historical perspective. One hundred and fifty years ago any discussion of rising sea levels would have focused on the shallow swamp called Back Bay. Then, the dominant industries of the day—mills and railroads—

invested to fill Back Bay with dams and reclaimed land. Beacon Street, which runs down the hill from where we are assembled today, ran across the top of a long and wide dam that was used to control the tides. Today, Back Bay is land, not water, and invulnerable to the tides. In fact, one-sixth of Boston's land area today is land that has been claimed from the seas. In the redevelopment of Boston harbor in the 1980s, planners factored in a likely rise in sea level—by preparing when they were already changing the landscape, Boston made itself more adaptive to climate change, at little cost. The "Big Dig," which put Boston's central road artery underground, is also constructed with the odds of higher seas in mind.

Every city with responsible leaders and a far-reaching vision has planned for such contingencies—London and Venice, for example, have movable sea walls to protect humanity's great physical assets from a flood tide. Such investments make sense even without global warming. Venice was already sinking into the ocean; its leaders have found a way to limit the danger of its natural sink and higher sea levels all at once.

We found that most claims of the high cost of climate change are built on a fallacy. They look only at losers and ignore the many winners. For every ski area that loses a day of sales from the earlier spring, global warming alarmists shed a tear and tabulate a cost. But they ignore the new business for fishing guides and outfitters, who can open earlier and close later. In fact, when Americans speak with their pocketbooks they prefer warm weather. They spend more on summer sports than those in the winter. Americans have moved in droves to warm weather. Even this audience of great Bostonians, I am sure, longs for a Florida respite in the dead of winter.

It is easy to be lighthearted about the weather, but I underscore a deadly serious point. We must be cautious about the "threat industry" that is drawn to the problem of global warming like termites to wood. A vast enterprise of analysts thrives—I dare say, draws its paycheck—from the exaggeration of environmental calamity. This same industry tells you that the streets are not safe, that prayer is corrupting, that the sky is falling. This same industry earns millions from malpractice lawsuits. They tell you that they are drawing your attention to problems; they say that they are making the world safer. But the reality is that it is you, the American consumer, who pays for them to tilt at windmills.

The threat industry draws its sustenance from fear. Its goal is self-propagation. Its standards are not rooted in the scrutiny, skepticism, and truth that are hallmarks of real science.

The threat industry has been working the climate case for decades. In the early 1970s analysts looked at the possibility of global cooling, triggered by grand plans at the time for a massive fleet of supersonic aircraft that would travel the globe. (Those plans were never realized because supersonic travel proved too costly; only the French and British Concorde program went ahead, and that only because those governments were willing to waste their taxpayers' money on a program for national pride.) Sure enough, when the doom patrol feared global cooling a plethora of detailed studies confirmed that cooling was bad news. Today the fear is warming and the studies show that warming is bad.

I have always found it puzzling why so many people who live in a country that has never been richer or more powerful are paralyzed by defeatism and malaise on environmental matters. Compare today with the turn of the twentieth century when soaring demand for wood fuel, railroad ties, and clear land for farming had denuded our forests and triggered fears of a "wood famine" in the United States. President Theodore Roosevelt created the U.S. Forest Service in 1905 to manage that strategic resource—to provide, in the words of the first Forest Service director, Gifford Pinchot, the "greatest good for the greatest number of people." Today, America's forests are larger and healthier because we have found ways to make productive use of our natural resources without overexploiting them. The effects are nowhere more visible than here in New England, where the countryside was virtually bare of trees a hundred years ago; today, healthy forests abound. Or, compare today with 1970, when President Richard Nixon's administration created the Clean Air Act, the Clean Water Act, and the National Environmental Policy Act—the most significant cluster of environmental legislation in our history. Or, compare today with slightly more than a decade ago when President George H.W. Bush oversaw the creation of a nationwide system for trading pollution credits that has cut in half the gases that cause acid rain. Today we are laying the groundwork to cut those emissions even further while also reducing other forms of pollution. Our long history of environmental achievements underscores that a healthy economy and respect for market forces are the best ways to protect nature.

That is what we have found in our review of the global warming problem. To be sure, our information is incomplete and there is more to do. We must constantly update our policy as new information arises. Let me outline the achievements that we are planning for the next months.

My administration will continue the bipartisan tradition of investing in the science of climate change. We must learn more about the risks and opportunities in a changing climate. Perhaps we will discover credible evidence of a looming danger. Until we have that evidence my administration will not impose such costs on the American economy. We are spending nearly $2 billion per year on climate science, focused on a wide range of important questions so that future leaders have better information for making these tough policy decisions.

We will continue to develop sensible policies that create incentives to reduce emissions where that can be achieved at little or no cost. We must ensure, however, that programs designed to acknowledge the voluntary efforts of firms do not merely deliver public relations benefits for things that firms would have done anyway. My administration is now implementing new rules that aim to reward only genuine reductions in emissions, and I commit here to review the effectiveness of those rules in the coming months.

My administration will continue to invest in the development of new technologies that might make it much less costly to reduce emissions in the future. It is essential that we have these options ready in case we find that steep cuts are needed; to a point, it makes sense to invest in research and development on these options now. These investments include the FutureGen program for coal-burning electric power generators, as well as a broad initiative to introduce hydrogen as a transportation fuel.

I don't know if these technology programs will pan out. That is the nature of bold technological investments—they are risky. We must expect failure but plan for success. I can assure you that these programs are already yielding important insights. We are working with industry so that the federal government is not given the task of paying the full cost and so that these programs are guided by practical considerations that industry knows best. We seek new technologies that work, not gold-plated behemoths that excite engineers but terrify hard-nosed businesspeople.

As we search for new energy systems, we must be mindful that real applications of technology depend on many factors, not just clever blueprints. We must create the market context that puts proper prices on energy and allows markets to transmit signals to final users. We must continue to introduce market forces in the supply of electricity. All these measures will create flexibility in the U.S. energy system, which is good news for the economy.

We must ensure that there are sufficient supplies of natural gas, a fuel that is intrinsically much less carbon-intensive than coal-fired electricity. Thus today I repeat my call for Congress to create the funding guarantees needed to encourage the private sector to build a gas pipeline to deliver the vast gas reserves in the North Slope of Alaska to markets here in the lower forty-eight states. Similarly, I applaud recent decisions by the Federal Energy Regulatory Commission to encourage the construction of liquefied natural gas receiving stations, which will help America overcome the crisis of high natural gas prices.

I am also issuing a series of executive orders that will help improve the nation's capacity to adapt to changing climate. I am directing the Federal Emergency Management Agency to review the practices that govern settlement of coastal zones. Already today, nature's normal pattern of surging seas and storms periodically causes great harm to coastal settlements, such as on the barrier islands off the Carolinas. Government must strike a balance in these areas. We must have compassion for the people affected by these disasters. But we must also avoid unwittingly creating an incentive for coastal dwellers to take risks with the government's money.

I am also directing the Federal Emergency Management Agency and other federal agencies to work with state and local authorities to be sure that the likely consequences of climate change are known—so that, where prudent, these factors can guide planning. In some cases it will make sense to build sea walls to fend off high sea levels and storms—almost always, the cases where such investments make sense are those in which such investments would be wise even without the risk of rising sea levels. Where we have already spent tens of billions of dollars on buildings near the coastline it makes sense to protect them against surging storms.

I would also like to outline some things that my administration won't do. For too long the policy response to global warming has been painted in stark, black-and-white terms. The threat industry has manufactured the terms of debate, and the noise has drowned voices of reason. In that polarized environment, analysts and politicians with special interests have brewed up a strong potion of mischief. My administration won't be serving that up.

I won't scare you with wild scenarios. Analysts have claimed that global warming will threaten America's security by spreading disease. Some claim, for example, that global warming will create malarial breeding grounds in the United States, implying that we will see a resurgence of that deadly disease here. The fact is that technology and policy are what determine the threat of malaria, not climate. During the Civil War the U.S. South was racked with malaria, driving up the world price for quinine, the only reliable treatment. Since then, programs to eradicate mosquitoes and control the disease explain why the South has long been malaria-free. The threat industry has concocted an endless array of other terrifying scenarios. I can't tell you that all are impossible. But I can say that the threat of climate change—like so many other policy challenges today—will require that we think in terms of probabilities. And the probabilities of these terror storylines are exceedingly low. We should spend our resources where the risks are greater.

I won't reengage with Kyoto. The problems with the Kyoto system are so severe that no amount of tinkering at the margins will fix them. It is hardly clear that substantial, coordinated reductions in emissions are needed. And the cost of meeting Kyoto's targets is way out of line with the treaty's minimal benefits. The most useful aspects of the Kyoto system envision engagement with developing countries; yet that system, known as the Clean Development Mechanism, has virtually no achievements to its credit. Environmentalists and European nations have burdened that mechanism with a plethora of special rules and procedures that make it difficult, if not impossible, for private firms to make the most sensible emission-reducing investments in developing countries. It is no wonder that developing countries have unanimously viewed this issue with suspicion—a plethora of promises but short on delivery. As a global strategy for tackling the problem of climate change, Kyoto is a backwater of costly paralysis and irrelevance.

Finally, I won't substitute government for your common sense. We will not construct elaborate government programs based on the idea that government is a nanny who must instruct you on the proper use of energy. Americans are smart. Armed with real information about real risks and rewards they will make sound choices. I view the role of government as helping, in those limited cases where markets fail, but leaving you—the consumer, parent, and steward—the freedom to choose.

In many ways the hypothetical dangers of climate change are, of course, quite different from the environmental problems that America has confronted in the past. The time scales are long; the causes are global; solutions are much more costly than anything else we have contemplated. But the global nature of climate change is not a reason for panic. In fact, we can handle these risks in our stride because the effects of a changing climate will unfold on the same time scale in which we will make many other changes in our society and technology. In the near future we have little control over the emissions that contribute to a changing climate, not least because many emissions come from other nations that are steadfast in their desire not to alter their behavior.

In short, we must learn, innovate, and adapt. We will invest in science so that we better understand the road ahead before we bet the economy on any radical course of action. We will invest in technology so that our society has the tools on hand should we need to cut our emissions in the future—and so that American workers and businesses stand ready to profit from innovation. All the while, we will prepare to adapt, just as Americans have adapted to many other environmental challenges in the past. These elements are not so much a clever strategy as just plain common sense.

SPEECH TWO: REINVIGORATING KYOTO

LOCATION: United Nations General Assembly, New York City

Mr. Secretary-General, Distinguished Delegates, and My Fellow Americans:

Today I speak with you about a grave threat to our prosperity. Addressing this challenge will tax our ability to work in unison as a community of nations. We must prevail, and time is short.

The danger is global climate change, and I come today to speak about why it is different from anything we have addressed before—and what it demands of us, the community of nations and citizens of the planet.

Climate change is unlike the threat of global nuclear war, a subject that occupied this body throughout the Cold War, because its solution does not lie merely in the hands of a few powerful states. Nor is climate change like most environmental problems in our past, which we have solved mainly by inventing new devices to bolt on our tailpipes and smokestacks. And the challenge of climate change is unlike terrorism, which we are addressing by working together to isolate and extinguish rogue elements.

Global climate change is different because the main cause—carbon dioxide from burning fossil fuels—is intrinsic to the metabolism of our modern economy. Fossil fuels power our prosperity. Fixing this problem requires rebuilding our industrial engine. The effort must be global, because all nations cause the emissions that lead to climate change. And we must find ways to make this transformation in a manner that is compatible with the markets and institutions that govern our industrial societies.

To start, we must understand why the challenge of climate change merits a response. One of many areas in which the United Nations system has provided leadership on this issue is in its creation, in 1988, of the Intergovernmental Panel on Climate Change—the IPCC.

[89]

This panel follows a long and distinguished tradition in the UN system of applying science to modern problems. The panel doesn't do the science, nor should it—the world's nations already amply fund and coordinate an impressive program of scientific research. The United States alone spends nearly $2 billion per year on climate science, and we will continue to increase our investment. The IPCC's contribution is to ensure a fair and balanced assessment by engaging thousands of scientists from around the world. The present head of the IPCC is an Indian economist; before him was an American atmospheric chemist who had been born in Britain, and the first head was a Swedish geochemist. The IPCC is the United Nations at its best—a vehicle for engagement and dialogue on the merits of ideas, regardless of nationality.

The message from the IPCC's admirable work is unmistakable. The problem of climate change is real. Temperatures are rising. The year 2003 was the third hottest on record; the 1990s were the hottest decade, by far, of the last one thousand years. Although changing temperatures are also the product of natural cycles, the human fingerprint is unmistakable.

It's not just temperature. Most other indicators of changing climate are also moving as the theory would expect. Satellites that are monitoring northern countries find that over just a decade the spring thaw has arrived a full week earlier, on average. Studies that have carefully culled the reports from thousands of amateur bird-watchers show that migratory birds arrive in their summer grounds earlier and leave later. In northern Alaska, the tundra once remained frozen solid for two hundred days per year; now that figure has dropped by half.

Looking to the future, the IPCC projects that sea levels probably will rise; areas prone to drought may become drier, and extreme storms may become more common. Natural ecosystems such as wetlands and forests, many already under stress, will be taxed even further.

In the past, many in the United States have shrugged off these likely effects. They say that we can adapt by changing our crops, shifting our houses inland away from the approaching sea, and building dikes to channel flood waters and irrigation to quench parched lands. I say that view is dangerously mistaken, and I intend to lead the United States to take action that addresses the root causes of climate change.

It is true that Americans can probably adapt to most of the likely short-term effects of climate change. One hundred miles southwest of here, the city of Philadelphia is planning for the possible need to relocate intake pipes for the water supply. Builders of new power plants near the coast have, in some cases, installed the intake pipes for coolant water a few feet higher than normal—in anticipation of higher future sea levels. But it is a stretch to say that merely moving a few pipes will make us immune to climate change. Our coastal zones are already battered by storms; rising sea level will make matters worse. In the barrier islands off the Carolinas and Florida, big storms already cause billions of dollars of property damage.

In most of the rest of the world such adaptation is not so easy. In Bangladesh alone nearly ten million people live within three vertical feet of sea level; Bangladeshis already suffer floods and devastation from coastal storms. Elsewhere in the developing world, societies that are least able to adapt to a changing climate are those that are on the front lines. These problems are serious for these societies, and they will affect us in the industrialized world as well—by creating environmental refugees, breeding grounds for climate-related diseases, and other stresses that will contribute to the same despair that has animated terrorists who have struck the United States.

Even as we struggle to protect the built environment from changing climate, what will we do about nature? For many ecosystems the rate of change that is likely to occur as the world warms will be much more rapid than nature's ability to adjust. Scientists studying unique ecosystems adapted to mountainous cloud forests in Costa Rica have shown that as temperatures rise, the clouds, too, will move higher up the mountain. What happens when they reach the top—when the clouds no longer shroud the forest? The cloud forest ecosystem disappears; butterflies and nature's other marvels go extinct. Ecologists are uncovering similar, detailed stories of stress and extinction everywhere that they look. Some have even suggested that perhaps one-third of species world-wide could go extinct in the coming century from the effects of global warming alone. That sounds abstract until you realize that coral reefs, wild forests, and many other gems of nature hang in the balance.

How should we evaluate such evidence? I worry that too many have focused on the integrity of the evidence itself. They have picked apart the studies by asking questions whose answers are not knowable. How do we know that the butterflies at the edge of extinction on one mountain do not survive somewhere else? Are we certain that exactly these effects will unfold in fifty years? What if some bird gets to the weakened butterflies first—are we, then, to blame for extinction? How do we know that future generations won't invent some clever device that will let us clone or move the butterflies to other mountains?

These are important questions. The nature of science is skepticism, and we must encourage scientists to turn every stone, question every fact, and re-question every hypothesis. We must be careful not to silence the skeptics—their criticism will make the science better.

But we, as planetary citizens, must also recognize the cost of indecision. Information is not free, and in this case the cost of waiting until all the facts are in is high indeed.

The very nature of the climate problem is one of uncertainty; the best information that we can expect is not declarative but a matter of probabilities. Climate change shifts the odds, but we will never be able to say that a particular hot summer or a particular extinction is the result of changing climate. It sounds like special pleading until you realize that practically every major decision taken by governments and firms is rooted in incomplete information.

Even more important than uncertainties are the irreversible effects. Not only are we saddling future generations with our effluent, but if they decide that they would have liked a world in which we did not drive to extinction one-third of nature's diversity there is nothing they can do to rewind the tape of history and play it again without our bad policies. It isn't right to impose those costs on the future. God did not put us on Earth to play dice with His legacy.

These factors taken together—the vulnerability of the world's poorest, the risk of catastrophic change, and our immoral legacy—are why we must eliminate the threats of climate change at their root. We must loosen and release the human grip on climate.

Carbon dioxide is the main cause of climate change, and most of that comes from burning fossil fuels such as coal, oil, and natural gas. Today, world emissions of carbon dioxide are about twenty-four billion tons per year, and they have been rising at nearly 1 percent per year on average for the last decade. As emissions rise, so does the concentration of carbon dioxide in the atmosphere. Today the atmosphere has about 380 parts per million of carbon dioxide—already one-third higher than the level at the onset of the industrial era.

A growing chorus of analysis suggests that the world should aim to stabilize the concentration at a level no higher than about 550 parts per million. To meet that goal we must not just slow the rise in emissions, we must actually reverse course—emissions must eventually be about 60 percent *lower* than they are today. And we must do that while allowing enough space in the global emission budget for the needs of developing countries. The United States and other industrialized nations have already amply used their shares of this budget; we must make a larger effort than the developing world. But all must play a role.

That level—550 parts per million—seems a long way off, but it is closer than you think. The climate system and the industrial energy system both have enormous inertia. To hit the 550 parts per million target by the end of the century, our trajectory of emissions must start shifting today—a little bit now, and a lot by 2020 and beyond. For the United States and other countries that must take the first steps, that means acting now: we must start by improving the efficiency of our existing energy system while laying the groundwork for a more radical transformation.

Few of the choices will be easy. For example, we must have debates about nuclear power—do we want more reactors, and where? Do we want more windmills and other carbon-free renewable power sources? If we build more gas-fired power plants in countries like the United States where gas is already scarce, where will we get the gas? Obtaining politically and economically viable answers to these questions takes time.

Every year that we wait to confront these questions is another year we lock ourselves into the old paradigm. Yet we know that business as usual is not sustainable. In 2003 the United States commissioned 402 new generating units with a total capacity of forty-four gigawatts. The largest of those plants will operate for thirty years; many will probably last even longer. The oldest grid-connected fossil fuel power plant in the United States was commissioned in the 1920s, and many small hydroelectric dams date from even earlier. We must be mindful of the durable consequences of our actions even today, and we must promote a similar awareness elsewhere in the world. Last year, China built thirty-two gigawatts of new power plants, and India built four gigawatts. The building will continue even more rapidly in the future. The International Energy Agency's authoritative *World Energy Outlook* suggests that two-thirds of the coal-fired electric power capacity that will exist in 2030 has not yet been built. Although we are locking in long-lived capital equipment, we still have room to maneuver if we act quickly.

Our response must be twofold. We must create a viable international institution for addressing the climate problem. And, within each nation, we must begin to implement concrete actions.

At the international level, I am mindful that the United States met a firestorm of criticism for leaving the Kyoto system. We did so because the Kyoto targets were not achievable. As the process of elaborating Kyoto's rules dragged on into 2001, the gap between U.S. emissions and the Kyoto limits grew so large that no viable policy could have delivered compliance for the United States. In that context, and with no comparable limits on emissions from developing countries, no American administration could have gained the legislative approval needed to put Kyoto into force. We bit off more than we could chew, and in that respect the United States was not alone. All nations have learned from the Kyoto experience. Continuing the effort in good faith is more important than whether our first try at creating an effective global institution to address one of the most complex issues on the international agenda was completely successful.

Looking to the future, we know that Kyoto is important for many other nations. We also know that Kyoto is the only established institution for addressing the climate issue. Thus today I am instructing our diplomats to engage fully with the Kyoto process, with the aim of achieving a viable plan for the United States to rejoin a system of binding commitments modeled after the Kyoto Protocol.

America's reengagement with Kyoto comes with strings attached. We will demand solutions to the flaws in the original Kyoto accords, and we will work with the community of nations to find fair and effective remedies. As we work to fix Kyoto, we will be mindful that well-meaning diplomats tried to achieve too much in the short term even as the Kyoto framework has proved to be woefully inadequate for the long term. We must rectify that imbalance. What matters most is a credible signal for long-term change. Our effort to establish long-term credibility requires achievable short-term milestones and accomplishments. We are lucky that the consequences of climate change will unfold over decades—giving us time, if we start now, to transform the global economy with the normal pace of technological change.

America will rejoin the Kyoto process only with solutions in hand for Kyoto's three deficiencies.

First, the new Kyoto must contain realistic targets with no free rides. The United States accounts for one-quarter of global emissions and therefore must do its share. Many, especially in this august body, have criticized America for its large environmental footprint, claiming that our consumer culture guzzles energy and intrinsically harms the environment. The reality is that America's emissions relative to economic output—what is often called "emission intensity"—are in line with those of most other nations. They are a bit higher than those of France and Japan, mainly because we use less nuclear power. They are lower than those of China, India, and South Africa. Like that of most nations, U.S. emission intensity is declining steadily over time.

The United States emits one-quarter of the world's carbon dioxide because we account for one-quarter of the world's economic output. Economic activity is not the enemy; it is essential to human welfare and to the technological innovation that is needed for an effective solution to the climate problem. It is the bedrock of development. What matters here is the trajectory of emissions—the path of emissions over time, and our success in decoupling emissions from economic growth. Every nation on Earth must strive for a low—eventually almost zero—emission intensity. We must have vibrant economies while stabilizing atmospheric concentrations at a safe level.

Reaching that safe level requires binding and stringent emission caps. That was the vision in Kyoto, and it must be the central element of an improved treaty as well. Voluntary limits are not enough.

With binding caps in place we can create an international emission trading system so that governments can meet the goal of protecting climate at the lowest possible cost. That concept was built into Kyoto and it must be reinvigorated.

In the new Kyoto we must also confront, head on, a subject that has been taboo: commitments for developing countries. As long as the community of developing nations is unified in rejecting any limits on emissions there will be no substantial progress in addressing the climate problem. And that is bad news especially for developing countries, as they—like most nations—stand to lose from unchecked global warming.

It will not be practical to set limits on emissions from all developing countries immediately. The wealthiest and largest must go first and clear a path for others. For those that do not adopt binding caps on their emissions we must find other ways of engagement so that they nonetheless have an incentive to reduce emissions and attract low-carbon technology and investment. In rejoining Kyoto, the United States will work to rewrite the rules for the Clean Development Mechanism so that it is more flexible and less bureaucratic. We are especially concerned that the present mechanism's rules provide few incentives to protect tropical forests, which are disappearing at a swift rate, a fact that is responsible for perhaps 20 percent of all the world's emissions of carbon dioxide.

Second, the new Kyoto must set realistic and meaningful long-term goals. No firm or government can plan a rational investment strategy without a star on the horizon to guide the effort. Over the last few months my administration has undertaken a comprehensive review of its policy strategy on global warming, and I have met personally and confidentially with the leaders of major energy companies. Most have expressed to me the need for clarity about goals. They say that if our climate policy consists of cutting emissions by possibly a few percent every five years then they will not much alter their business plans. They will install technologies that are a bit more efficient because energy efficiency, to a point, is the cheapest source of carbon savings available. They will invest in projects overseas where substantial reductions in emissions are achievable at very low cost.

But we must signal that our goal is a radical reduction in emissions, requiring a greater response from business. Even today, if our aspirations were clear, some utilities would build new nuclear plants while others would invest in larger wind farms. A clear and credible vision would uncork innovation in zero-carbon energy systems, such as the elements of a hydrogen-based energy system. Some firms are investing in these futures, but the effort is much too tentative. The job of government is not to pick the winners in this battle for new energy systems; rather, our task is to set and enforce the goals.

In setting goals we must send a clear and unambiguous message: we seek nothing less radical than the decarbonization of the world economy. We will need fifty years or longer to achieve that goal. I commend Britain's prime minister for outlining a vision for the transformation of his nation's economy; the U.S. government, in the coming months, will do the same.

[97]

I propose that we start with 550 parts per million of atmospheric carbon dioxide as a goal. We should write that number prominently into the new Kyoto agreement, and we should also create a process for evaluating and adjusting that goal regularly. Whenever we set emission targets we should convene a group of experts—with the help of the Intergovernmental Panel on Climate Change—to tell us whether the emissions pathways we are envisioning are consistent with our goals. I know that this statement will be seen by many, especially in the scientific community, as foolhardy. How do we know that 550 parts per million is safe? We don't, and we may never know what is safe. But we do have a good idea about the rates and magnitude of change implied by this target, and I am confident that the 550 goal is achievable at acceptable cost.

I can assure you that once we have penciled in this number, a flood of studies will follow to show why it is deficient. That, exactly, is the dialectical process that we must inspire.

Third, the new Kyoto must recognize that the only viable way to decarbonize the economy is to develop and install new technologies. Even with a credible long-term goal, the needed investment will not flow automatically. Many of the new ideas that will be needed to decarbonize the economy are public goods—everyone in the world will benefit from these new ideas, but no single firm or government can justify the costly investment on its own. We know that society tends to underinvest in knowledge and other public goods, and in this case the underinvestment is truly global.

In the present Kyoto regime there is no reward for nations that invest in such public goods. Indeed, a system that sets new targets every five years actually discourages some technological investments because a nation that lowers its emission trajectory puts itself at a disadvantage for later rounds of negotiations. We must eliminate these perverse incentives and create a strong, direct incentive for productive investment in new technology.

Our leaders in business and government must work together to set the exact form of this technology investment program. At minimum, a credible technology strategy will require governments not only to subsidize the development of new technologies; they must also cap emissions so that there is a strong incentive for firms to deploy new technologies. We must establish a process of peer review that encourages each nation to look closely at the technology investment plans in the private and public sectors of other countries so that a better, coordinated international strategy emerges. We must create international mechanisms for collaborative research on new large-scale technologies, such as strategies for making clean renewable power widely available. And we must not forget the continual need for the invention and application of technologies that boost energy efficiency.

In addition to invigorating a new Kyoto, my administration is also committing the United States to a more aggressive course of domestic policy. We will demonstrate our dedication to creating an effective international response through our own substantial response at home. Our policy will include five major elements.

First, we will complete the installation of an effective voluntary system for registering reductions in emissions. We need stricter accounting standards so that this registry does not simply reward firms for projects they would have undertaken anyway. A voluntary approach is not enough, but it is what we have right now. It is available immediately to help jump-start a mandatory, economy-wide response. My administration will explore whether firms that make reductions now might get special allocations in a future emission trading system, which would create a strong incentive for early action.

Second, the U.S. government will encourage—where it can— the many special programs that encourage low-cost ways to control emissions. I am always amazed when I hear stories such as the ability of BP to cut its emissions of carbon dioxide by 10 percent while actually creating $650 million in new value for the firm's shareholders. In economics you learn that there aren't any $100 bills lying on the street because if there were, people would pick them up. From my experience talking with industry leaders, the street is filled with $100 bills, and we just need to learn how to find and grab them. Some firms are already doing this. Government can help with informational programs that aid other firms in starting the search. Government—including local government—can also help households with the search. About one-third of the energy consumed in the United States is used in households, and many studies have shown that homeowners are typically unaware of how they can save money (and cut emissions) through more efficient appliances, upgraded insulation, low-energy lighting, and other simple changes.

Third, my administration will introduce legislation to create a binding emission trading system for all significant sources of carbon dioxide in the United States. Senators John McCain and Joe Lieberman have proposed such legislation; I will work with them to build on their efforts.

Our binding trading system will start with carbon dioxide because it is the easiest to measure, but we will include other gases in the future as it becomes easier to monitor them reliably— exactly as the European Union is doing in its own emission trading system. Until then, we will regulate these other gases through effective voluntary and mandatory programs that we have already demonstrated in practice. They include the Environmental Protection Agency's programs to encourage capture of methane from landfills, its partnership with the aluminum industry for reducing emissions of strong greenhouse gases called perfluorocarbons, its "Gas Star" program that has worked with the gas industry to cut venting and leaking from the nation's natural gas infrastructure, and many other programs.

We must put a priority on finding ways to measure and reward those who alter land use practices so that soils store more carbon. Enormous quantities of carbon and topsoil have been lost from deep plowing and runoff; yet there is good evidence that widespread use of "no till" farming as well as better forest management practices can boost the ability of land to sequester carbon in the soils and in plants. Success in such efforts will broaden the coalition of those who favor action to include the many states in America that are rich in farms and forests.

Fourth, we will redouble our investment in new technology. We will expand our programs to develop and deploy renewable power and ultra-efficient energy systems. The United States has also launched programs to develop the technologies that will be needed for a zero-carbon hydrogen energy system, and we welcome the many private initiatives in this area as well. From India to Iceland we have found enormous interest in joint international exploration of this promising hydrogen future. Governments that are serious about addressing the climate change problem know that technology is the key. I am encouraged by evidence that hard-nosed venture capitalists are also putting more money into clean energy systems.

With industry, the U.S. government is supporting the demonstration of an advanced coal gasification power plant—what we call FutureGen—that will make it possible to generate electricity from coal while capturing and sequestering the carbon dioxide underground. If we apply that technology to burning biomass we could create the world's first substantial energy source that has negative emissions of carbon dioxide. Growing biomass removes CO_2 from the atmosphere, and the FutureGen approach can then park the carbon away forever.

These are a start. The U.S. government will spend $4 billion on incentives to apply climate-friendly technologies this year. We will do more. We also expect that private sector firms will do more—much more—when they see a credible signal that the world and the United States are serious about cutting carbon. We must realize that effective technology policy requires strong incentives for business to put new technologies into practice. A binding cap on emissions is that incentive.

Fifth, we will continue to invest in scientific research on the causes and consequences of climate change because sound science is essential to sound policy. Already the United States spends about $2 billion per year on climate science. We fly satellites and plumb the depths of the oceans for clues about past, current, and future climates. Nearly all that work is done in partnership with other nations. We contribute mightily to the Intergovernmental Panel on Climate Change. While sustaining and increasing this investment, we must also be sure that the many uncertainties in the science do not become an excuse for inaction. We must look at the likely effects of climate change, and we must be especially focused on spotting the possibly catastrophic consequences. More work is needed to understand and predict those effects, as they will dominate our attempts to avoid danger by setting and sustaining a safe level of greenhouse gases in the atmosphere.

Finally, I must emphasize that America knows that climate change does not allow America to be a political island. We must engage with other nations in truly collaborative fashion.

Two decades ago, this body—the United Nations General Assembly—created a commission to study the fate of the global environment. The result, chaired by Norwegian Prime Minister Gro Brundtland, was an impressive report that bears revisiting. It offers a vision for improving human welfare while also protecting the environment, which it called "sustainable development." The Brundtland Commission argued that the environment and the economy were complementary, not contradictory. "Our common future," the commission said, required assuring that each generation passes the planet to the next with its vital resources intact.

We must reaffirm the Brundtland vision by addressing the danger of climate change with a truly global and long-term strategy that befits the problem at hand. If we are to ensure our prosperity for our children we must not wait. I stand before you to assure you that, when focused on effective solutions to climate change, the United States will be at the forefront in reinvigorating that global effort.

SPEECH THREE: MAKING A MARKET

LOCATION: Portland, Oregon

My Fellow Americans:

I have spent the day traveling the Columbia River. I have retraced the route of Lewis and Clark and met small business owners and citizens here in Oregon and in Washington. They have shared with me their aspirations and visions. Many have discussed their fears as well, especially their concerns about the natural environment. Many have told me that environmental quality is why they are here. For a large fraction, the environment is their livelihood. They are outfitters and innkeepers and farmers. The environment, they say, is luxury and necessity all in one.

Over the last two centuries our modern society has confronted and solved many environmental problems. Nearly all these have been local or regional in nature. About one hundred years ago this great nation faced a terrible timber crisis. Railroads and farmers, especially in the East, were cutting trees much more rapidly than the forests could recover. We solved the crisis by creating the U.S. Forest Service to manage the forests and by supporting programs that helped farmers learn to grow more food on less land. Similarly, we have largely solved the local pollution problems that, until recently, bedeviled city life. From contamination of the water supplies to killer smog, we have risen to the challenge. Today, we are cutting emissions of sulfur dioxide, nitrogen oxides, and mercury from power plants. We are working to reduce emissions of fine particulates, which have proved to be more dangerous to human health than previously thought. For those who claim that environmental quality is in perpetual decline, I say look at the record. It is quite impressive. We have caused real harm, but we have also found real solutions.

Now we confront the problem of climate change. I am not exaggerating when I say that this is today's most serious long-term threat to environmental quality. I will not recount the evidence in detail, but you have all heard it. Global temperatures are rising now and will rise further. Weather patterns will change. Sea level is likely to rise, at least a bit, and storms may become more intense. The stress of a changing climate will alter natural ecosystems, driving perhaps many species into extinction.

Most of these changes in climate are the result of human actions, mainly the emission of carbon dioxide, which is a byproduct of burning fossil fuels.

You will see the effects of climate change right here. Warmer temperatures are likely to reduce snowpack. More water will flow down the Columbia in winter—when it otherwise would have been locked up in snow and ice on the mountains—and less in summer. Electricity prices may rise, since the water for Bonneville and other dams along the river is much more valuable in summer, when demand for electricity is growing as more people install air conditioners. Hot summer temperatures will probably affect fish in rivers and the rest of nature. Such effects, though varied, will be felt anywhere and everywhere on Earth. For perhaps the first time in history, there is no place on Earth where humans can experience a pristine environment; the signature of mankind's pollution of carbon dioxide and other greenhouse gases is truly pervasive.

It is safe to say that we don't know the exact consequences of a changing climate. But it is also safe to say that we know enough to be worried and to take precautionary action now.

Today, I'd like to outline the response that we—as Americans and as citizens of Earth—should pursue. Our effort must begin here at home. Only with credible programs in place can we lead the world.

We will be successful in solving the problem of climate change only with new thinking about the role of government in the economy. We will never find cost-effective solutions if we think about carbon dioxide and other greenhouse gases the way we have traditionally thought about pollutants—with mandates for end-of-pipe technologies. We must create new markets with strong incentives for private firms and individuals to invent radically new methods for supplying energy services. It probably means, over fifty years, building a new economy that relies far less on fossil fuels.

To understand the magnitude of the task, imagine your day without fossil fuels. No car; no electricity in most of the country; no air travel; no gas for cooking and heating. Obviously we can't make the shift overnight. Luckily, climate change is the result of a slow accumulation of greenhouse gases in the atmosphere. So long as we don't squander our time, the atmosphere can afford the fifty years that we will need to make the change in our energy systems.

There are great dangers in undertaking this transformation of our economy. The costs could be enormous if we adopt foolish policies, such as mandates for firms and households to adopt particular technologies. Some say that we should not pay attention to cost because the urgent needs of planet Earth must come first. I don't think that is realistic—we must pay attention to cost because a program that imposes an excessive burden will not sustain the political support that is necessary to be effective.

For those who care most passionately about solving the global warming problem, I warn you: ill-conceived remedies that are not politically sustainable can cause even more harm than inaction. The United States government left the Kyoto Protocol on global warming precisely because we consented in Kyoto to commitments that outstripped what we could reasonably deliver. When key countries exit, the regime founders.

The only way to make this transformation is through the market itself. The market must reflect the real cost of carbon dioxide. Today, the price of gasoline made from oil or of electricity made from coal does not reflect the burdens of global warming. How can we get the prices right?

We can start by not getting prices wrong. The energy industry is second only to agriculture in the level of subsidy that all of us taxpayers provide. We deliver subsidies directly. We also indirectly distort energy markets, for instance by providing free protection in sea lanes for oil tankers. Because of those subsidies we have succumbed to pressure to subsidize new entrants as well—in a costly effort to re-level the playing field. Thus today we not only subsidize fossil fuels but also wind and solar and nuclear energy. We invent reasons for still more subsidies—we subsidize ethanol, a liquid fuel made from corn, in part on the fiction that ethanol-blended fuels are a cost-effective way to clean the air. We let automakers get special fuel efficiency credits when they manufacture vehicles that can burn ethanol and other locally manufactured fuels, on the logic that such fuels do not require us to import oil—yet few of those vehicles, in practice, burn anything but the same oil-based fuels that the rest of us put in our tanks. Our government can't afford these subsidies, and they undermine the principles of free-market environmentalism that will boost our economic productivity even as we protect nature. We must work with other countries to narrow then stop all subsidies for energy.

To go further—beyond removing insidious subsidies—we must create new policy instruments. For several decades this country has experimented with market-based mechanisms for controlling pollution. The best model is the highly successful program that we adopted in 1990 to control emissions of sulfur dioxide, the leading cause of acid rain. In that case, we cut emissions in half by imposing a cap on all the major sources and then letting firms trade emission credits. Some firms found inexpensive ways to apply new technology, giving them surplus credits to sell or bank for the future. Others bought credits rather than install technologies that were not cost-effective. The incentive to control emissions spurred innovation—proof that environmentalism can go hand in hand with innovation and strong economies.

My administration is making much greater use of markets for controlling many other forms of pollution as well. We are building on the work of several northeastern states to create a market in nitrogen oxides; we are also creating a new market in mercury emissions. Although much of the federal government's efforts to protect the environment still employ traditional "command and control" methods—where government, in essence, tells you which technologies and processes are best—we are making progress in the shift to market-based strategies. You may not know it, but the results are visible all around and even in your pocketbook. Good studies by serious economists have shown that these market-based approaches typically cut pollution for about half the cost of traditional government regulation. That leaves more resources for the environment and the economy.

We must create an emission trading system for carbon. Unlike the federal government's current voluntary efforts, America must have a binding system that strives to include all sources, so that no firm or family is disadvantaged. But we must be mindful that many fluxes of greenhouse gases are hard to measure; we must discount those to ensure that our trading system has integrity and to create incentives to develop better systems for monitoring. We must pay particular attention to the opportunity for changing land use practices so that our soils absorb more carbon. Low-till agriculture, integrated land management, and reforestation are among the many ways that farmers and foresters can do their part while gaining credit. Not only is this good for climate, but it will also help to slow soil erosion and protect biological diversity.

The federal effort must begin modestly. Senators McCain and Lieberman proposed a bill that made a good start, and I support it. The federal effort must not supplant important action in the states. Oregon is at the forefront of those efforts. You have set voluntary targets for reducing emissions. You have formed a pact with Washington and British Columbia to pursue a regional strategy for controlling emissions, and complementary efforts in California are leading to a western states approach. Nearly all the states in the Northeast are working together to develop a trading system for emissions of carbon dioxide from power plants. Some of these efforts reflect frustration that the federal government has not done more. But some also reveal keen interest in experimenting with new ideas and concepts that, eventually, could be woven into a broader program. I applaud that. As in so many other areas of American policy, the state laboratories of federalism are essential to our success in identifying the best policy strategies for the nation.

That logic is fine enough, but global warming is a global problem. What should be done in the rest of the world? We must not have any illusions. If we do not have a credible answer to this question we are unlikely to solve the problem of global warming.

For the last decade the countries that have cared most about solving the global warming problem have tried to create a global regime for capping the emissions of greenhouse gases, as well as an international system for emission trading. They have worked "top down," and the most visible product of their venture is the Kyoto Protocol.

The Kyoto vision has not worked. For one, the cost of meeting any demanding treaty obligation that includes emission trading is extremely sensitive to the actions of many other governments working in concert. Yet concerted action is extremely difficult to achieve under international law as each nation's interests and circumstances change with time. In the case of the United States, the caps were set at a moment when America's diplomats were unaware of how rapidly our emissions would rise and how much it would cost to comply.

Kyoto's architects imagined that all nations would participate and move in lockstep. All would measure compliance with the same metrics; all would recognize, broadly, the same trading rules. That's a tall order under international law—where enforcement provisions are weak and prone to becoming politicized. And it is a dangerous, unrealistic vision because it creates treaties that are prone to unzip—as Kyoto has done.

As the years rolled by, it became increasingly impossible to attain the Kyoto limits. When the United States exited the value of emission credits that Russia had hoped to sell us plummeted. As the Russians wavered it became less likely that Kyoto would ever enter into force as a binding treaty. With Kyoto then hanging in the balance, developing countries found that the rush of investment and new technology promised in the Kyoto bargain did not materialize as expected.

This top-down vision is particularly problematic because it is hardly clear how to set the best rules. Some nations want to encourage the protection of tropical forests. Others are opposed—they want to keep pressure for transformation focused on the energy system, where emissions are larger and easier to measure. Some want to give credit for nuclear power; others not. In the top-down system all these disagreements must be worked out in advance of the trading system actually operating, with little practical experience to guide the design.

For too long we have thought about this task as an environmental problem. The real nature of our challenge is little different from inventing a new form of money—a carbon currency. Eventually, when the carbon market takes hold, everyone will examine the carbon consequences of their actions, just as everyone today thinks about the capital requirements of their behavior, whether it is building a new factory, buying a car, or constructing a home.

In creating a strong carbon currency we must get the rules right at home. And we must work with nations that are committed to ensure that carbon emission credits have real value. All the while, we must ensure that government does its best to stay out of the way as markets find their prices.

We can start by establishing a trading system here in the United States. Europe has already offered its vision in its own trading system. Canada is exploring a similar move; we should urge Japan, also, to look at using markets to cut carbon and other greenhouse gases. We have an interest in other countries' establishing effective trading systems, and they have an interest in our doing the same.

As each creates its own sound trading system the zone for trading will grow and so will the gains from trade. The emergence of different zones will allow us to discover which countries are managing their new currency well. We will trade with them. We will scrutinize those that are printing extra permits and adopting procedures that undermine the strong currency. With them, we will allow trade at a discount or not at all. At the center of this evolving system will be the world's largest market—the United States.

Through our policies and our decisions about which permits to honor we can assure that the nascent international emission trading system is built on effective and efficient rules. In doing that, we must work with Europe and Japan to expand the size of the market and assure a strong currency. Together, we can guarantee the integrity of the global effort.

This view will be controversial. For too long those who have accepted the need for serious action to slow global warming have also assumed that a top-down international treaty was the only solution. Yet the lessons of history suggest that the most effective international institutions begin with the efforts of a small like-minded core.

Consider the World Trade Organization—today's most effective and successful example of international regime building. The WTO did not spring forth from a top-down vision for international trade. Rather, it was built up through a series of bilateral agreements that were packaged together into a truly multilateral approach known as the General Agreement on Tariffs and Trade. Eventually the WTO emerged, and each member of the WTO has been expected to adopt a long and complex series of commitments. It would have been impossible to impose such sophisticated and interlocking commitments on the WTO's members if the trade regime had not first built experience and confidence with less intrusive and more decentralized rules.

This alternative organic vision helps us to focus on what we must do now. In the Kyoto system, most experts have anticipated that trading would begin with Russia and the developing countries. Those countries offer the greatest opportunity for low-cost emission controls. But these countries are also least likely to create a sound currency. With few exceptions, they do not have the legal and regulatory institutions in place to assure adequate enforcement. In the case of developing countries, the Kyoto approach doesn't even cap emissions, making it essentially impossible to know whether emission reductions are genuine. A much better strategy would create a zone of trust first with the countries that we know share our interests and have the capacity to support sound money. The

European system offers the best opportunity for exchange. It is built on a solid foundation and backed with vigorous enforcement.

Some will criticize this vision as too slow and too small. They will say that we must start with all nations—including developing nations and Russia. They will also say that we must move rapidly.

But we must not underestimate the difficulty of creating a new international currency. The European Union has recently created a new international currency, the euro. That has been a long and arduous process: enforcement has proved difficult when powerful countries such as France and Germany violate the rules. Keeping the system on an even keel has proved difficult, even though the Europeans have created a strong new central bank especially to manage the euro.

We must not underestimate the risk to our prosperity and to our success in slowing global warming if we get this wrong. We cannot afford to include in our new currency nations and markets that will undermine integrity, just as we do not tolerate those who counterfeit our dollars. Prosperity requires credibility and confidence in the rules that govern the economy. I can assure you that there is no faster way to erase, with great pain, our diligent efforts at slowing global warming than to hurriedly create a system that will come unraveled when some unscrupulous trader in a distant land is given the opportunity to attack.

Even as we work with a small group of countries to create a strong currency, we must not ignore the imperative to control emissions worldwide. Indeed, the stronger our effort the greater the need for those outside the zone—notably Russia and the developing countries—to make their contribution as well. We in the industrialized world care most about this issue and we have caused most of the problem, and thus we must lead. But we must also be vigilant in ensuring that the cost of action does not tilt the playing field of economic competition too steeply against us, as that will make it harder to sustain the political will needed for this great transformation in our economy.

We can do two things to engage the rest of the world. First, we can put all on notice that they will soon be expected to join the strong trading system that the United States and like-minded allies are building. Indeed, we will explore a wide array of strong incentives—including sanctions, which have worked in other international environmental arrangements—to ensure that, eventually, no nation gets a free ride. If we make a severe effort to cut emissions we should even explore making access to our market conditional upon others making comparable efforts.

I propose that we start with our own program—on a trial basis for 2008–2012 and in full operation for the years 2012–17, which dovetails neatly with the European emission trading system. We will work with other nations in the zone to build a nascent international trading system. For the period after 2017 we will expect the biggest and wealthiest developing nations—Brazil, China, India, Mexico, and South Africa among them—to join the system. I will work with Congress and with the leaders of other nations to reach agreement on the exact targets and timetables for action.

Second, in the interim, we have an obligation to work with Russia and developing countries on broad programs for controlling emissions. Already there are many opportunities for controlling emissions that are in these countries' interest and could be pursued more rapidly. They include plugging the holes in the Russian gas pipeline network. They include the efforts in most countries—including China and India—to make greater use of natural gas instead of coal. Gas emits just half the carbon dioxide per unit of useful energy that coal does. When China builds its gas network it will lock itself into a future energy system that is cleaner. That is good for China, good for the world, and good for the nations—from Australia to Indonesia to Russia—that sell gas to China. We can encourage that shift by sharing information about gas networks and ensuring that private investors in the gas business have fair access to the Chinese market.

We must not pretend that our effort to build a strong currency will advance by awarding piles of emission credits as inducements for China, Russia, or any other nation that is not part of our currency zone. How many credits should China get because it builds its gas network? Should we reward Russia with emission credits just because its economy has collapsed and it is investing in projects, such as energy efficiency, that make sense anyway? These difficult questions have been a mainstay of debate in the Kyoto system, and they have led diplomats to concoct a Kyoto trading mechanism that will be tied in red tape.

Already Kyoto has created something called the Clean Development Mechanism that issues credits project by project for investments in developing countries. The idea was to reward investors whose actions reduced emissions to a level lower than would have occurred otherwise. That was an admirable idea at the time, but it has proved unworkable because the most important investments for reducing long-term emissions—such as building gas networks to displace coal—are not discrete activities for which it is possible to make an unambiguous determination of credits. It is telling that the Clean Development Mechanism, while slated to start four years ago, has made barely any progress in awarding real credits.

The programmatic efforts that I propose are a better alternative. They will help put developing countries on better pathways. They will also help us grow climate-friendly export businesses. Our task as policymakers and citizens is to create a practical system and then to let our market-based economy do what it does best—invent and apply solutions.

We can be successful in this effort, but only if we do not tilt at false windmills. With Kyoto we have tried both too much and too little. We have not paid close enough attention to creating a robust system first here in the United States. We have not explored adequately ways to work with our allies—especially in Europe—to create a system here that links with the trading system that is already taking shape over there. And we must ensure that we do not frustrate these fragile but important efforts by loading ever larger subsidies on the already grossly distorted economics of energy.

I am confident that when we get the incentives right, solving the climate problem will be much easier and less expensive than we think. The key to our success lies in adopting the right models as we invent this new currency. With sustained effort we can, indeed, transform our energy system—and the world's—in time to check the worst of global warming.

We need a century to see the full fruit of our efforts. To gain confidence in our success, look back one hundred years and see how much has changed. You would see no highways and essentially no automobiles. Average life expectancy was three decades shorter than today's seventy-seven years; nine-tenths of doctors had no college education, and only 8 percent of households had a telephone. And back two hundred years you would not have heard yet of Lewis and Clark. With the right time horizon in mind we can channel the vibrant innovation that has made the American economy strong and will make our environment cleaner as well.

APPENDIXES

APPENDIX A: SENATE DEBATE OVER THE BYRD-HAGEL RESOLUTION, JULY 25, 1997

In July 1997, before the final negotiations on the Kyoto Protocol, Senators Robert Byrd (D-WV) and Chuck Hagel (R-NE) sponsored a resolution, which passed by a vote of 95-0, declaring that the Senate would reject any treaty that did not require "new specific scheduled commitments to limit or reduce greenhouse gas emissions for Developing Country Parties within the same compliance period." The resolution also vowed to reject any treaty that would cause "serious harm" to the U.S. economy. The "sense of the Senate" debate held before the resolution was adopted revealed a wide range of interpretations of the resolution's sparse language—especially concerning the requirements for developing country commitments. Reproduced below are the full text of the resolution and excerpts from the debate on July 25, 1997. For the full debate, go online to http://thomas.loc.gov/cgi-bin/query/z?r105:S25JY7-15:

S. RES. 98 (BYRD-HAGEL RESOLUTION)
105th Congress, 1st Session, July 25, 1997

Whereas the United Nations Framework Convention on Climate Change (in this resolution referred to as the 'Convention'), adopted in May 1992, entered into force in 1994 and is not yet fully implemented;

Whereas the Convention, intended to address climate change on a global basis, identifies the former Soviet Union and the countries of Eastern Europe and the Organization For Economic Co-operation and Development (OECD), including the United States, as 'Annex I Parties', and the remaining 129 countries, including China, Mexico, India, Brazil, and South Korea, as 'Developing Country Parties';

Whereas in April 1995, the Convention's 'Conference of the Parties' adopted the so-called 'Berlin Mandate';

Whereas the 'Berlin Mandate' calls for the adoption, as soon as December 1997, in Kyoto, Japan, of a protocol or another legal instrument that strengthens commitments to limit greenhouse gas emissions by Annex I Parties for the post-2000 period and establishes a negotiation process called the 'Ad Hoc Group on the Berlin Mandate';

Whereas the 'Berlin Mandate' specifically exempts all Developing Country Parties from any new commitments in such negotiation process for the post-2000 period;

Whereas although the Convention, approved by the United States Senate, called on all signatory parties to adopt policies and programs aimed at limiting their greenhouse gas (GHG) emissions, in July 1996 the Under Secretary of State for Global Affairs called for the first time for 'legally binding' emission limitation targets and timetables for Annex I Parties, a position reiterated by the Secretary of State in testimony before the Committee on Foreign Relations of the Senate on January 8, 1997;

Whereas greenhouse gas emissions of Developing Country Parties are rapidly increasing and are expected to surpass emissions of the United States and other OECD countries as early as 2015;

Whereas the Department of State has declared that it is critical for the Parties to the Convention to include Developing Country Parties in the next steps for global action and, therefore, has proposed that consideration of additional steps to include limitations on Developing Country Parties' greenhouse gas emissions would not begin until after a protocol or other legal instrument is adopted in Kyoto, Japan in December 1997;

Whereas the exemption for Developing Country Parties is inconsistent with the need for global action on climate change and is environmentally flawed;

Whereas the Senate strongly believes that the proposals under negotiation, because of the disparity of treatment between Annex I Parties and Developing Countries and the level of required emission reductions, could result in serious harm to the United States economy, including significant job loss, trade disadvantages, increased energy and consumer costs, or any combination thereof; and

Whereas it is desirable that a bipartisan group of Senators be appointed by the Majority and Minority Leaders of the Senate for the purpose of monitoring the status of negotiations on Global Climate Change and reporting periodically to the Senate on those negotiations: Now, therefore, be it

Resolved, That it is the sense of the Senate that—

(1) the United States should not be a signatory to any protocol to, or other agreement regarding, the United Nations Framework Convention on Climate Change of 1992, at negotiations in Kyoto in December 1997, or thereafter, which would—

(A) mandate new commitments to limit or reduce greenhouse gas emissions for the Annex I Parties, unless the protocol or other agreement also mandates new specific scheduled commitments to limit or reduce greenhouse gas emissions for Developing Country Parties within the same compliance period, or

(B) would result in serious harm to the economy of the United States; and

(2) any such protocol or other agreement which would require the advice and consent of the Senate to ratification should be accompanied by a detailed explanation of any legislation or regulatory actions that may be required to implement the protocol or other agreement and should also be accompanied by an analysis of the detailed financial costs and other impacts on the economy of the United States which would be incurred by the implementation of the protocol or other agreement.

Sec. 2. Secretary of the State shall transmit a copy of this resolution to the President.

EXPRESSING SENSE OF SENATE REGARDING UN FRAMEWORK
CONVENTION ON CLIMATE CHANGE
(SENATE—JULY 25, 1997)

MR. CHUCK HAGEL (R-Nebraska). [...] The Byrd-Hagel resolution is a strong bipartisan wake-up call to the administration.

This resolution rejects the United Nations' current negotiating strategy of binding the United States and other developed nations to legally binding reductions without requiring any new or binding commitments from 130 developing nations, such as China, Mexico, and South Korea. In addition, this resolution rejects any treaty or other agreement that would cause serious economic harm to the United States.

[...] Mr. President, this makes no sense, no sense at all, given that these nations include some of the most rapidly developing economies in the world and are quickly increasing their use of fossil fuels. By the year 2015, China will surpass the United States as the largest producer of greenhouse gases in the world.

[...] If these nations are excluded, greenhouse gas emissions will continue to rise, and we would see no net reductions in global greenhouse gas emissions. The exclusion of these nations is a fatal flaw in this treaty.

[...]

MR. ROBERT C. BYRD (R-West Virginia). [...] I do not think the Senate should support a treaty that requires only half the world—in other words, the developed countries—to endure the economic costs of reducing emissions while developing countries are left free to pollute the atmosphere and, in so doing, siphon off American industries. There are those who say that the United States is responsible for the situation that has developed. They claim that the United States should bear the brunt of the burden. But the time for pointing fingers is over. In this particular environmental game there are no winners; the world loses. And any effort to avoid the effects of global climate change will be doomed to failure from the start without the participation of the developing world, particularly those nations that are rapidly developing and will rapidly increase their carbon dioxide and other greenhouse gas emissions.

[...] The concept which is embodied in the Byrd-Hagel resolution is that developing country parties should join the developed world in making new specific scheduled commitments to limit or reduce greenhouse gas emissions within the same compliance period.

Now, does this mean that the Senate is insisting on commitments to identical levels of emissions among all the parties? Certainly not. The emissions limitations goals, to be fair, should be based on a country's level of development. The purpose is not to choke off Mexico's development or China's development. The purpose is to start addressing the greenhouse gas problem in the only meaningful way we can, that is, through globally and through binding commitments up front. The timeframe could be 5 years, 7 years, 10 years or whatever. The initial commitment to action, starting upon signature in Kyoto, could be relatively modest, pacing upwards depending upon various factors, with a specific goal to be achieved within a fixed time period. There are plenty of tools to encourage the developing world to make meaningful commitments.

[...] American industry has expressed concern that a treaty without developing country commitments would encourage capital flight and a loss of jobs in the United States. We do not as yet have available the administration's current best assessment of the economic impacts of various levels of emissions targets in the United States. However, preliminary work done by the Argonne Laboratory on this matter is worrisome in that its worst case scenario shows a very negative economic impact on American industry.

[...] Now, some of the Senators who have signed on to the resolution may have differing views about the treaty, but there is one thing that we are in agreement on—one or two things. These are set forth in the resolution beginning and concluding with the resolving clause. One, that all nations, all nations must take steps now, at the time of the signing of the treaty, to begin limiting their emissions of greenhouse gases. Mere promises will not be sufficient. Mere promises will not get by this Senate. A treaty will have to have the approval of a two-thirds supermajority in this Senate, and that is what we are telling the administration. We are letting the administration know that this Senate is not just going to consent or not consent on a treaty. This Senate is going to fulfill its constitutional obligations not only to consent but also to 'advise' and consent. And the resolution also provides that such a treaty must not result in serious harm to the economy of the United States.

[...]

MR. JOHN F. KERRY (D-Massachusetts). [...] That common sense is the notion that if you are really going to do something to affect global climate change and you are going to do it in a fair-minded way that will permit you to build consensus in the country, which is important, and to build the necessary support to ratify a treaty, we are going to have to do this in a way that calls on everybody to share the burden of responding to this problem. That means that we need to have an agreement that does not leave enormous components of the world's contributors and future contributors of this problem out of the solution.

[...] Let me point out a couple of those areas where we had some concerns. There is language in the resolution about the developing nations accomplishing their reductions within exactly the same compliance period as the developed nations. I have come to the conclusion that these words are not a treaty killer that some suggested it might have been.

[...] There still appears to be a little bit of uncertainty as to what this phrase within the same compliance period actually means. But after a number of discussions with Senator Chafee's and Senator Byrd's staffs, I believe that we have reached an understanding that it means essentially that we want countries to begin to reduce while we are reducing, we want them to engage in a reasonable schedule while we are engaged in a reasonable schedule, but that if a developing nation needs more time to get a plan in place or needs to have more time to raise the funds and be able to purchase the technology and do the things necessary, that as long as there is a good-faith track on which they are proceeding, that if it took them a number of years, 2 years, 3 years, 5, or longer to be able to reach a particular goal, that certainly means within the same compliance period they are operating similarly to try to meet the standards that we want to set out. We believe that, given that less-developed countries are not currently projected to emit more emissions than industrial countries until at least the year 2015, it is reasonable to permit some flexibility in the targets and the timing of compliance while at the same time requiring all countries to agree to make a legally binding commitment by a date certain.

That is reasonable. But I think most of my colleagues would agree that if some country simply doesn't have the capacity, the plan, the money, or the technology, it may be they have to take a little more time and we should want to be reasonable in helping them to do that because the goal here is to get everybody to participate, not to create a divisiveness that winds up with doing nothing.

[…] Emissions trading not only advantages the U.S. business, but it would provide developing countries with incentives to sign up to binding legal commitments that most people believe are important in this treaty.

[…]

MR. TRENT U. LOTT (R-Mississippi). […] And what would the developing nations contribute? What would our neighbors in Mexico have to do to help stop global warming? Nothing. What about other so-called developing nations like Korea, China, India, and Brazil? The treaty lets them off the hook. Mr. President, this is not an equitable international policy. This is not a level playing field for the United States.

[…] The Byrd-Hagel resolution would require developing nations to comply with the same regulations at the same time in the same treaty as the United States. This is not only equitable, it is the only way that there can be any real benefit to the global environment.

[…]

MR. A. MITCH MCCONNELL (R-Kentucky). […] The Byrd-Hagel resolution addresses the unfairness in the agreement being considered by the administration. This resolution mandates specific scheduled commitments to limit or reduce greenhouse gas emission for developing nations, with the same compliance period.

If every nation doesn't agree to the same emission levels and timetables, what incentive will they have to negotiate in the future when they have an overwhelming competitive advantage? It is important that we not bargain away the economic advantages we have worked so hard to achieve.

[…]

MR. MAX S. BAUCUS (D-Montana). […] The language contained in Senate Resolution 98 will help achieve the goal of including all countries in the new treaty.

It requires that the treaty mandate new specific scheduled commitments to limit or reduce greenhouse gas emissions for developing country parties within the same compliance period as developed countries.

But since developing and developed nations are starting from different places, it makes sense to require different targets. Here again, the language crafted by Senator Byrd helps. It does not specify that developed and developing countries meet the same targets and timetables.

[…] So although the language of the resolution requires new commitments from developing countries, the administration should seek emission targets that are more consistent with their level of industrialization.

[…]

MR. JON L. KYL (R-Arizona). […] While I presume many supporters of this resolution agree that under no circumstances should the United States be subjected to legally binding emissions limitations, I believe the resolution is somewhat unclear. As I read it, it says the United States will agree to legally binding emissions if 'the protocol or other agreements also mandates new specific scheduled commitments to limit or reduce greenhouse gas emissions for developing country parties within the same compliance period.' Unfortunately, I believe this condition is not sufficient. As many of you know, it has been interpreted by different people in different ways. Some read it to mean that the Senate will not approve a treaty that does not include identical emissions level and target date requirements. Others, however, have read the same language and determined that it means any treaty must have equal commitments when it comes to setting timetables but not emissions levels. Unfortunately, it is easy to set developing countries on a timetable and allow them to continue to pollute in any amount they desire. The emissions levels can be easily set so that the developed countries have very stringent, and perhaps unattainable levels, while the developing countries have very lax, easily reached goals—all the while, all countries are operating within the same timetable.

[…] This approach, I believe, defeats the purpose of the treaty ratified by the Senate, which is to voluntarily reduce greenhouse-gas emissions on a global scale. The original intent was not to legally bind the Annex I countries to set timetables and emissions levels while only requiring the developing countries to comply with parallel timetables but not the same emissions standards.

[…]

MR. J. ROBERT KERREY (D-Nebraska). […] The resolution before us requires commitments of developing countries to mitigate greenhouse gas emissions in the same timeframes as developed countries. This may resonate as promoting a policy that discourages the participation of many developing countries. However, the resolution will allow developing countries appropriate flexibilities in commitments to address global climate change abatement. The United States and other developed countries must accord newly developed and developing countries flexibilities and incentives to participate, and these need not create economic disadvantages to the United States or any other developed country.

I cannot emphasize enough the importance of this point. Without all countries on board, inaction becomes inevitable, because emission reductions achieved by one country will soon be offset by increased emissions from another.

An equitable approach that encourages commitments by all parties and that offers incentives to developing countries is needed. Market-based solutions to curb emissions will allow continued economic growth with minimal impacts. Developed countries are in a better position to implement emissions-curbing activities and technologies at low cost and impact, and to also transfer these abilities and technologies to developing countries and to aid in their economic advancement in a way that tempers emissions growth.

While measures to stabilize greenhouse gases at a certain level will inevitably lead to some energy price increases, an international emissions-trading scheme could substantially reduce the potential costs. What is needed, however, is a policy to ensure that incremental costs of reducing or stabilizing emissions are equalized across firms, across sectors, and across countries. This can only occur if we take into account the economies, emissions and abilities of countries to participate, and if we assign actions accordingly and in appropriate timeframes.

Market mechanisms can reduce cost impacts of emissions reductions agreements. A preferable policy would be to set short- and long-term goals to stabilize greenhouse gas emissions, and to set quantity limits on emissions that are linked to prices. Targets and timetables for emission limitations cannot operate independently of market prices. An international tradeable emissions permits system, with price caps and floors, would have revenue potential and would be cost-efficient.

[…]

MR. JOSEPH I. LIEBERMAN (D-Connecticut). […] New commitments by developing countries regarding their performance under the Framework Convention on Climate Change, of course, need to be consistent with their historic responsibility for the problem, as well as their current capabilities.

[…] The resolution says that developing countries can start with a commitment that is lower relative to the industrialized countries at first. Over time, however, the commitments of developing and developed countries must become comparable to ensure that every country does its fair share to address the problem.

Senate Resolution 98 states that developing countries have to start making quantified emissions reductions objectives within the same compliance period as developed countries. This means that at a stage to be negotiated over the compliance period of the Kyoto agreement, developing countries must begin to make quantified emissions reductions objectives. Senate Resolution 98 says that it is entirely appropriate for industrialized countries to start making quantified emissions reductions first, as long as developing countries also commit to making quantified emissions reductions before the end of the time period worked out for the Kyoto agreement.

[...]

MR. JEFF BINGAMAN (D-New Mexico). [...] The central issue for us today is the role that the United States and other developed countries will play in any effort to control greenhouse gas emissions, compared to the role that developing countries will play. Here, too, the administration has shown considerable sophistication, compared to other parties in the negotiations. All developing countries are not alike—there is a world of difference between South Korea and Gambia, despite the fact that both are non-Annex-I countries. The world should expect more from South Korea, which aspires to join the OECD in the near future, than it should from Gambia. But there should also be a minimum level of expectations mandated by the upcoming agreement, even for countries like Gambia.

I believe that a careful examination of the proposal put forward by the administration shows that it is trying to make these principles part of the protocol.[1] We should go on record, in this res-

---

[1] The administration's negotiating position for Kyoto had been expressed, *inter alia*, by Timothy E. Wirth, Undersecretary for Global Affairs, Department of State, who testified on Thursday, June 18, 1997.

"[...] We have proposed three separate elements for developing countries in our proposal for Kyoto:

"1. We call on developing countries to continue to elaborate on their commitments in the Convention—including by providing information on emissions on an annual basis (the same as for developed countries), and by taking "no regrets measures" (actions which may be valuable in their own right, and which also mitigate climate change). We also call for a regular review of the actions developing countries are taking (again, using a review process similar to that established to assess our own actions).

"2. We call on the newly developed countries (such as Mexico and Korea) to take on binding legal obligations to reduce emissions, recognizing that while the targets they adopt may not be the same as our own, such commitments will codify their new status, and differentiate them from the lesser developed countries.

"3. We call for the negotiation of a new legal instrument which will include legally binding obligations for all countries—including all developing countries—as a next step in the path toward the ultimate stabilization of greenhouse gas concentrations in the atmosphere at a level that is not dangerous."

olution, in support of such principles. But we need to do so in a careful and sophisticated way, befitting the complexities of the problem of human-induced global climate change, and the international policy response to it.

I did not cosponsor the resolution that is now before us because of my concerns about how it expressed the relationship between what the United States should do and what the developing countries should do. It used the words 'new commitments' for both developed and developing countries in a way that suggested to me, at least, that the intent of the resolution was that the United States should not agree to any commitment that was not also going to be agreed to and implemented simultaneously by the world's poorest countries. That would seem to be a rather simplistic approach. We shouldn't ignore legitimate differences between countries at vastly different stages of development.

[…] I would like to engage in a colloquy with the senior Senator from West Virginia regarding the correct interpretation of the language of the resolution on one particular point of importance. The resolution refers to 'new commitments to limit or reduce greenhouse gas emissions for the Annex I Parties' as well as to 'new specified scheduled commitments to limit or reduce greenhouse gas emissions for Developing Country Parties.' Would it be correct to interpret the use of the words 'new commitments' in both phrases as suggesting that the United States should not be a signatory to any protocol unless Annex I Parties and Developing Country Parties agree to identical commitments?

MR. ROBERT C. BYRD (R-West Virginia). That would not be a correct interpretation of the resolution. In my testimony before the Committee on Foreign Relations on June 19, I made the following statement and deliberately repeated it for emphasis: 'Finally, while countries have different levels of development, each must make unique and binding commitments of a pace and kind consistent with their industrialization.' I believe that the developing world must agree in Kyoto to binding targets and commitments that would begin at the same time as the developed world in as aggressive and effective a schedule as possible given the gravity of the problem and the need for a fair sharing of the burden. That is what the resolution means. The resolution should not be interpreted as a call for identical commitments between Annex I Parties and Developing Country Parties.

[...] Mr. President, I will try to elaborate on my view with a two-part observation. First, with respect to significant emitters, such as China, it makes no sense for the international community to begin this effort by agreeing to unchecked emissions growth from newly constructed, but inefficient, power-generating and industrial facilities. It is neither cost-effective nor environmentally beneficial to go back and retrofit dirty smokestacks.

We all know that China in particular has near-term plans to increase its power-generating capacity exponentially. We must anticipate the prospect of significant new industrial development in China and other places by providing incentives for deployment of new, cleaner technologies. In short, we must bring back from Kyoto some commitments that China and other large emitters will grow in a smart way.

I want to make it clear that the current approach of the State Department is not acceptable to this Senator under the terms of the resolution. Their approach will not work. A promise by the developing countries to only negotiate at a later date is simply unacceptable. Any agreement resulting from negotiations in Kyoto, or thereafter, that includes binding commitments for developed countries must also include serious, specific, and binding commitments by the developing world.

APPENDIX B: NATIONAL ASSESSMENT OF THE POTENTIAL CONSEQUENCES OF CLIMATE VARIABILITY AND CHANGE, OVERVIEW CONCLUSIONS, 2000

In 1997 the Clinton administration asked the United States Global Change Research Program (USGCRP) to conduct a comprehensive assessment of the possible consequences of climate change and options for easing adaptation. The study and the resulting report, "The 2000 National Assessment of the Potential Consequences of Climate Variability and Change," were managed by the National Assessment Synthesis Team (NAST)—a committee of experts from government, academia, industry, and NGOs. Climate models provided a range of possible global and regional changes in temperature, precipitation, water levels, forest growth, and other sensitive areas; for example, the report assumes that the accumulation of greenhouse gases in the atmosphere would cause temperatures in the United States to rise between 5 and 9 degrees Fahrenheit (3–5 degrees Celsius) in the next 100 years.

What follows are main conclusions from the Assessment's "Foundation Report," published in 2000 and written by the NAST in cooperation with independent regional organizations. The complete reports are available online at http://www.usgcrp.gov/usgcrp/nacc/default.htm

Climate Change Impacts on the United States: The Potential Consequences of Climate Variability and Change, Overview Conclusions

Large Impacts in Some Places
The impacts of climate change will be significant for Americans. The nature and intensity of impacts will depend on the loca-

tion, activity, time period, and geographic scale considered. For the nation as a whole, direct economic impacts are likely to be modest. However, the range of both beneficial and harmful impacts grows wider as the focus shifts to smaller regions, individual communities, and specific activities or resources. For example, while wheat yields are likely to increase at the national level, yields in western Kansas, a key US breadbasket region, are projected to decrease substantially under the Canadian climate model scenario. For resources and activities that are not generally assigned an economic value (such as natural ecosystems), substantial disruptions are likely.

Multiple-stresses Context

While Americans are concerned about climate change and its impacts, they do not think about these issues in isolation. Rather they consider climate change impacts in the context of many other stresses, including land-use change, consumption of resources, fire, and air and water pollution. This finding has profound implications for the design of research programs and information systems at the national, regional, and local levels. A true partnership must be forged between the natural and social sciences to more adequately conduct assessments and seek solutions that address multiple stresses.

Urban Areas

Urban areas provide a good example of the need to address climate change impacts in the context of other stresses. Although large urban areas were not formally addressed as a sector, they did emerge as an issue in most regions. This is clearly important because a large fraction of the US population lives in urban areas, and an even larger fraction will live in them in the future. The compounding influence of future rises in temperature due to global warming, along with increases in temperature due to local urban heat island effects, makes cities more vulnerable to higher temperatures than would be expected due to global warming alone. Existing stresses in urban areas include crime, traffic congestion, compromised air and water quality, and disruptions of personal and business life due to decaying infrastructure. Climate change is likely to amplify some of these stresses, although all the interactions are not well understood.

Impact, Adaptation, and Vulnerability

As the Assessment teams considered the negative impacts of climate change for regions, sectors, and other issues of concern, they also considered potential adaptation strategies. When considered together, negative impacts along with possible adaptations to these impacts define vulnerability. As a formula, this can be expressed as vulnerability equals negative impact minus adaptation. Thus, in cases where teams identified a negative impact of climate change, but could not identify adaptations that would reduce or neutralize the impact, vulnerability was considered to be high. A general sense emerged that American society would likely be able to adapt to most of the impacts of climate change on human systems but that the particular strategies and costs were not known.

Widespread Water Concerns

A prime example of the need for and importance of adaptive responses is in the area of water resources. Water is an issue in every region, but the nature of the vulnerabilities varies, with different nuances in each. Drought is an important concern in every region. Snowpack changes are especially important in the West, Pacific Northwest, and Alaska. Reasons for the concerns about water include increased threats to personal safety, further reduction in potable water supplies, more frequent disruptions to transportation, greater damage to infrastructure, further degradation of animal habitat, and increased competition for water currently allocated to agriculture. The table below illustrates some of the key concerns related to water in each region.

WATER ISSUES						
Region	Floods	Droughts	Snowpack/Snowcover	Groundwater	Lake, River, and Reservoir Levels	Quality
Northeast	X	X	X	X		X
Southeast	X	X		X		X
Midwest	X	X	X	X	X	X
Great Plains	X	X	X	X	X	X
West	X	X	X	X	X	X
Northwest	X	X	X		X	
Alaska		X	X			
Islands	X	X		X		X

Note: This table identifies some of the key regional concerns about water. Many of these issues were raised and discussed by stakeholders during regional workshops and other Assessment meetings held between 1997 and 2000.

Health, an Area of Uncertainty

Health outcomes in response to climate change are highly uncertain. Currently available information suggests that a range of health impacts is possible. At present, much of the US population is protected against adverse health outcomes associated with weather and/or climate, although certain demographic and geographic populations are at greater risk. Adaptation, primarily through the maintenance and improvement of public health systems and their responsiveness to changing climate conditions and to identified vulnerable subpopulations should help to protect the US population from adverse health outcomes of projected climate change. The costs, benefits, and availability of resources for such adaptation need to be considered, and further research into key knowledge gaps on the relationships between climate/weather and health is needed.

Vulnerable Ecosystems

Many US ecosystems, including wetlands, forests, grasslands, rivers, and lakes, face possibly disruptive climate changes. Of everything examined in this Assessment, ecosystems appear to be the most vulnerable to the projected rate and magnitude of climate change, in part because the available adaptation options are very limited. This is important because, in addition to their inherent value, they also supply Americans with vital goods and services, including food, wood, air and water purification, and protection of coastal lands. Ecosystems around the nation are likely to be affected, from the forests of the Northeast to the coral reefs of the islands in the Caribbean and the Pacific.

ECOSYSTEM GOODS & SERVICES

Ecosystem	Goods	Services
Forests	Timber, fuelwood, food such as honey, mushrooms, and fruits	Purify air and water, generate soil, absorb carbon, moderate weather extremes and impacts, and provide wildlife habitat and recreation
Freshwater Systems	Drinking and irrigation water, fish, hydroelectricity	Control water flow, dilute and carry away wastes, and provide wildlife habitat, transportation corridors, and recreation
Grasslands	Livestock (food, game, hides, fiber), water, genetic resources	Purify air and water, maintain biodiversity, and provide wildlife habitat, employment, aesthetic beauty, and recreation
Coastal Systems	Fish, shellfish, salt, seaweeds, genetic resources	Buffer coastlines from storm impacts, maintain biodiversity, dilute and treat wastes, and provide harbors and transportation routes, wildlife habitat, employment, beauty, and recreation
Agro-ecosystems	Food, fiber, crop genetic resources	Build soil organic matter, absorb carbon, provide employment, and provide habitat for birds, pollinators, and soil organisms

ECOSYSTEM VULNERABILITY

Ecosystem Type	Impacts	NE	SE	NW	GP	WE	PNW	AK	IS
Forests	Changes in tree species composition and alteration of animal habitat	X	X	X		X	X	X	X
	Displacement of forests by open woodlands and grasslands under a warmer climate in which soils are drier		X						
Grasslands	Displacement of grasslands by open woodlands and forests under a wetter climate					X			
	Increase in success of non-native invasive plant species				X	X	X		X
Tundra	Loss of alpine meadows as their species are displaced by lower-elevation species	X				X	X	X	
	Loss of northern tundra as trees migrate poleward							X	
	Changes in plant community composition and alteration of animal habitat							X	
Semi-arid and Arid	Increase in woody species and loss of desert species under wetter climate					X			
Freshwater	Loss of prairie potholes with more frequent drought conditions				X				
	Habitat changes in rivers and lakes and amount and timing of runoff changes and water temperatures rise	X	X	X	X	X	X		
Coastal and Marine	Loss of coastal wetlands as sea level rises and coastal development prevents landward migration	X	X			X	X		X
	Loss of barrier islands as sea-level rise prevents landward migration	X	X						
	Changes in quantity and quality of freshwater delivery to estuaries and bays alter plant and animal habitat	X	X			X	X	X	X
	Loss of coral reefs as water temperature increases		X						X
	Changes in ice location and duration alter marine mammal habitat							X	

Note: The table above gives a partial list of potential impacts for major ecosystem types in various regions of the U.S. While the impacts are often stated in terms of what is likely to happen to plant communities, it is important to recognize that plant-community changes will also affect animal habitat.

Agriculture and Forestry Likely to Benefit in the Near Term
In agriculture and forestry, there are likely to be benefits due to climate change and rising CO_2 levels at the national scale and in the short term under the scenarios analyzed here. At the regional scale and in the longer term, there is much more uncertainty. It must be emphasized that the projected increases in agricultural and forest productivity depend on the particular climate scenarios and assumed CO_2 fertilization effects analyzed in this Assessment. If, for example, climate change resulted in hotter and drier conditions than projected by these scenarios, both agricultural and forest productivity could possibly decline.

Potential for Surprises
Some of the greatest concerns emerge not from the most likely future outcomes but rather from possible "surprises." Due to the complexity of Earth systems, it is possible that climate change will evolve quite differently from what we expect. Abrupt or unexpected changes pose great challenges to our ability to adapt and can thus increase our vulnerability to significant impacts.

A Vision for the Future
Much more information is needed about all of these issues in order to determine appropriate national and local response strategies. The regional and national discussion on climate change that provided a foundation for this first Assessment should continue and be enhanced. This national discourse involved thousands of Americans: farmers, ranchers, engineers, scientists, business people, local government officials, and a wide variety of others. This unique level of stakeholder involvement has been essential to this process, and will be a vital aspect of its continuation. The value of such involvement includes helping scientists understand what information stakeholders want and need. In addition, the problem-solving abilities of stakeholders have been key to identifying potential adaptation strategies and will be important to analyzing such strategies in future phases of the assessment.

The next phase of the assessment should begin immediately and include additional issues of regional and national importance including urban areas, transportation, and energy. The process should be supported through a public-private partnership. Scenarios that explicitly include an international context should guide future assessments. An integrated approach that assesses climate impacts in the context of other stresses is also important. Finally, the next assessment should undertake a more complete analysis of adaptation. In the current Assessment, the adaptation analysis was done in a very preliminary way, and it did not consider feasibility, effectiveness, costs, and side effects. Future assessments should provide ongoing insights and information that can be of direct use to the American public in preparing for and adapting to climate change.

APPENDIX C: NATIONAL ACADEMY OF SCIENCES, "CLIMATE CHANGE SCIENCE: AN ANALYSIS OF SOME KEY QUESTIONS," EXECUTIVE SUMMARY, 2001

In the wake of the U.S. withdrawal from the Kyoto Protocol in 2001, the Bush administration asked the National Academy of Sciences to address several key questions regarding the scientific understanding of climate change. In addition, the administration asked the NAS to review the recently released Third Assessment Report from the Intergovernmental Panel on Climate Change, the main intergovernmental body that is tasked to review scientific issues surrounding climate change. Notably, the administration asked the NAS to examine the integrity of the IPCC's detailed reports as well as whether there were substantive differences between those detailed reports and the IPCC's shorter "Summary for Policy Makers."

The executive summary from the National Academy of Sciences report (Climate Change Science: An Analysis of Some Key Questions) *follows and is reprinted by courtesy of the National Academies Press, Washington, DC. The full text is available for purchase from the press or free online at: http://books.nap.edu/books/0309075742/html/*

SUMMARY

Greenhouse gases are accumulating in Earth's atmosphere as a result of human activities, causing surface air temperatures and subsurface ocean temperatures to rise. Temperatures are, in fact, rising. The changes observed over the last several decades are likely mostly due to human activities, but we cannot rule out that some significant part of these changes is also a reflection of natural vari-

[138]

ability. Human-induced warming and associated sea level rises are expected to continue through the 21st century. Secondary effects are suggested by computer model simulations and basic physical reasoning. These include increases in rainfall rates and increased susceptibility of semi-arid regions to drought. The impacts of these changes will be critically dependent on the magnitude of the warming and the rate with which it occurs.

The mid-range model estimate of human-induced global warming by the Intergovernmental Panel on Climate Change (IPCC) is based on the premise that the growth rate of climate forcing[2] agents such as carbon dioxide will accelerate. The predicted warming of 3°C (5.4°F) by the end of the 21st century is consistent with the assumptions about how clouds and atmospheric relative humidity will react to global warming. This estimate is also consistent with inferences about the sensitivity[3] of climate drawn from comparing the sizes of past temperature swings between ice ages and intervening warmer periods with the corresponding changes in the climate forcing. This predicted temperature increase is sensitive to assumptions concerning future concentrations of greenhouse gases and aerosols. Hence, national policy decisions made now and in the longer-term future will influence the extent of any damage suffered by vulnerable human populations and ecosystems later in this century. Because there is considerable uncertainty in current understanding of how the climate system varies naturally and reacts to emissions of greenhouse gases and aerosols, current estimates of the magnitude of future warming should be regarded as tentative and subject to future adjustments (either upward or downward).

Reducing the wide range of uncertainty inherent in current model predictions of global climate change will require major advances

---

[2]A climate forcing is defined as an imposed perturbation of Earth's energy balance. Climate forcing is typically measured in watts per square meter (W/m^2).

[3]The sensitivity of the climate system to a prescribed forcing is commonly expressed in terms of the global mean temperature change that would be expected after a time sufficiently long for both the atmosphere and ocean to come to equilibrium with the change in climate forcing.

in understanding and modeling of both (1) the factors that determine atmospheric concentrations of greenhouse gases and aerosols, and (2) the so-called "feedbacks" that determine the sensitivity of the climate system to a prescribed increase in greenhouse gases. There also is a pressing need for a global observing system designed for monitoring climate.

The committee generally agrees with the assessment of human-caused climate change presented in the IPCC Working Group I (WGI) scientific report, but seeks here to articulate more clearly the level of confidence that can be ascribed to those assessments and the caveats that need to be attached to them. This articulation may be helpful to policy makers as they consider a variety of options for mitigation and/or adaptation. In the sections that follow, the committee provides brief responses to some of the key questions related to climate change science. More detailed responses to these questions are located in the main body of the text.

What is the range of natural variability in climate?

The range of natural climate variability is known to be quite large (in excess of several degrees Celsius) on local and regional spatial scales over periods as short as a decade. Precipitation also can vary widely. For example, there is evidence to suggest that droughts as severe as the "dust bowl" of the 1930s were much more common in the central United States during the 10th to 14th centuries than they have been in the more recent record. Mean temperature variations at local sites have exceeded 10°C (18°F) in association with the repeated glacial advances and retreats that occurred over the course of the past million years. It is more difficult to estimate the natural variability of global mean temperature because of the sparse spatial coverage of existing data and difficulties in inferring temperatures from various proxy data. Nonetheless, evidence suggests that global warming rates as large as 2°C (3.6°F) per millennium may have occurred during retreat of the glaciers following the most recent ice age.

Are concentrations of greenhouse gases and other emissions that contribute to climate change increasing at an accelerating rate, and are different greenhouse gases and other emissions increasing at different rates? Is human activity the cause of increased concentrations of greenhouse gases and other emissions that contribute to climate change?

The emissions of some greenhouse gases are increasing, but others are decreasing. In some cases the decreases are a result of policy decisions, while in other cases the reasons for the decreases are not well understood.

Of the greenhouse gases that are directly influenced by human activity, the most important are carbon dioxide, methane, ozone, nitrous oxide, and chlorofluorocarbons (CFCs). Aerosols released by human activities are also capable of influencing climate. (Table 1 lists the estimated climate forcing due to the presence of each of these "climate forcing agents" in the atmosphere.)

Concentrations of carbon dioxide (CO_2) extracted from ice cores drilled in Greenland and Antarctica have typically ranged from near 190 parts per million by volume (ppmv) during the ice ages to near 280 ppmv during the warmer "interglacial" periods like the present one that began around 10,000 years ago. Concentrations did not rise much above 280 ppmv until the Industrial Revolution. By 1958, when systematic atmospheric measurements began, they had reached 315 ppmv, and they are currently ~370 ppmv and rising at a rate of 1.5 ppmv per year (slightly higher than the rate during the early years of the 43-year record). Human activities are responsible for the increase. The primary source, fossil fuel burning, has released roughly twice as much carbon dioxide as would be required to account for the observed increase. Tropical deforestation also has contributed to carbon dioxide releases during the past few decades. The excess carbon dioxide has been taken up by the oceans and land biosphere.

Like carbon dioxide, methane (CH_4) is more abundant in Earth's atmosphere now than at any time during the 400,000 year long ice core record, which dates back over a number of glacial/interglacial cycles. Concentrations increased rather smoothly by about

1% per year from 1978, until about 1990. The rate of increase slowed and became more erratic during the 1990s. About two-thirds of the current emissions of methane are released by human activities such as rice growing, the raising of cattle, coal mining, use of land-fills, and natural gas handling, all of which have increased over the past 50 years.

A small fraction of the ozone (O_3) produced by natural processes in the stratosphere mixes into the lower atmosphere. This "tropospheric ozone" has been supplemented during the 20th century by additional ozone, created locally by the action of sunlight upon air polluted by exhausts from motor vehicles, emissions from fossil fuel burning power plants, and biomass burning.

Nitrous oxide (N_2O) is formed by many microbial reactions in soils and waters, including those acting on the increasing amounts of nitrogen-containing fertilizers. Some synthetic chemical processes that release nitrous oxide have also been identified. Its concentration has increased approximately 13% in the past 200 years.

Atmospheric concentrations of CFCs rose steadily following their first synthesis in 1928 and peaked in the early 1990s. Many other industrially useful fluorinated compounds (e.g., carbon tetrafluoride, CF_4, and sulfur hexafluoride, SF_6), have very long atmospheric lifetimes, which is of concern, even though their atmospheric concentrations have not yet produced large radiative forcings. Hydrofluorocarbons (HFCs), which are replacing CFCs, have a greenhouse effect, but it is much less pronounced because of their shorter atmospheric lifetimes. The sensitivity and generality of modern analytical systems make it quite unlikely that any currently significant greenhouse gases remain to be discovered.

What other emissions are contributing factors to climate change (e.g., aerosols, CO, black carbon soot), and what is their relative contribution to climate change?

Besides greenhouse gases, human activity also contributes to the atmospheric burden of aerosols, which include both sulfate particles and black carbon (soot). Both are unevenly distributed, owing to their short lifetimes in the atmosphere. Sulfate particles scatter solar radiation back to space, thereby offsetting the green-house effect to some degree. Recent "clean coal technologies" and use of low sulfur fuels have resulted in decreasing sulfate concentrations, especially in North America, reducing this offset. Black carbon aerosols are end-products of the incomplete combustion of fossil fuels and biomass burning (forest fires and land clearing). They impact radiation budgets both directly and indirectly; they are believed to contribute to global warming, although their relative importance is difficult to quantify at this point.

How long does it take to reduce the buildup of greenhouse gases and other emissions that contribute to climate change? Do different greenhouse gases and other emissions have different draw down periods?

TABLE 1

Removal Times and Climate Forcing Values for Specified Atmospheric Gases and Aerosols

Forcing Agent	Approximate Removal Times*	Climate Forcing (W/m²) up to the Year 2000
Greenhouse Gases		
Carbon Dioxide	> 100 years	1.3 to 1.5
Methane	10 years	0.5 to 0.7
Tropospheric Ozone	10–100 days	0.25 to 0.75
Nitrous Oxide	100 years	0.1 to 0.2
Perfluorocarbon Compounds	>1000 years	0.01
(Including SF₆)		
Fine Aerosols		
Sulfate	10 days	−0.3 to −1.0
Black Carbon	10 days	0.1 to 0.8

*A removal time of 100 years means that much, but not all, of the substance would be gone in 100 years. Typically, the amount remaining at the end of 100 years is 37%; after 200 years 14%; after 300 years 5%; after 400 years 2%.

Is climate change occurring? If so, how?

Weather station records and ship-based observations indicate that global mean surface air temperature warmed between about 0.4 and 0.8°C (0.7 and 1.5°F) during the 20th century. Although the magnitude of warming varies locally, the warming trend is spatially widespread and is consistent with an array of other evidence detailed in this report. The ocean, which represents the largest reservoir of heat in the climate system, has warmed by about 0.05°C

(0.09°F) averaged over the layer extending from the surface down to 10,000 feet, since the 1950s.

The observed warming has not proceeded at a uniform rate. Virtually all the 20th century warming in global surface air temperature occurred between the early 1900s and the 1940s and during the past few decades. The troposphere warmed much more during the 1970s than during the two subsequent decades, whereas Earth's surface warmed more during the past two decades than during the 1970s. The causes of these irregularities and the disparities in the timing are not completely understood. One striking change of the past 35 years is the cooling of the stratosphere at altitudes of ~13 miles, which has tended to be concentrated in the wintertime polar cap region.

Are greenhouse gases causing climate change?

The IPCC's conclusion that most of the observed warming of the last 50 years is likely to have been due to the increase in greenhouse gas concentrations accurately reflects the current thinking of the scientific community on this issue. The stated degree of confidence in the IPCC assessment is higher today than it was 10, or even 5 years ago, but uncertainty remains because of (1) the level of natural variability inherent in the climate system on time scales of decades to centuries, (2) the questionable ability of models to accurately simulate natural variability on those long time scales, and (3) the degree of confidence that can be placed on reconstructions of global mean temperature over the past millennium based on proxy evidence. Despite the uncertainties, there is general agreement that the observed warming is real and particularly strong within the past 20 years. Whether it is consistent with the change that would be expected in response to human activities is dependent upon what assumptions one makes about the time history of atmospheric concentrations of the various forcing agents, particularly aerosols.

By how much will temperatures change over the next 100 years, and where?

Climate change simulations for the period of 1990 to 2100 based on the IPCC emissions scenarios yield a globally-averaged surface temperature increase by the end of the century of 1.4 to 5.8°C (2.5 to 10.4°F) relative to 1990. The wide range of uncertainty in these estimates reflects both the different assumptions about future concentrations of greenhouse gases and aerosols in the various scenarios considered by the IPCC and the differing climate sensitivities of the various climate models used in the simulations. The range of climate sensitivities implied by these predictions is generally consistent with previously reported values.

The predicted warming is larger over higher latitudes than over low latitudes, especially during winter and spring, and larger over land than over sea. Rainfall rates and the frequency of heavy precipitation events are predicted to increase, particularly over the higher latitudes. Higher evaporation rates would accelerate the drying of soils following rain events, resulting in lower relative humidities and higher daytime temperatures, especially during the warm season. The likelihood that this effect could prove important is greatest in semi-arid regions, such as the U.S. Great Plains. These predictions in the IPCC report are consistent with current understanding of the processes that control local climate.

In addition to the IPCC scenarios for future increases in greenhouse gas concentrations, the committee considered a scenario based on an energy policy designed to keep climate change moderate in the next 50 years. This scenario takes into account not only the growth of carbon emissions, but also the changing concentrations of other greenhouse gases and aerosols.

Sufficient time has elapsed now to enable comparisons between observed trends in the concentrations of carbon dioxide and other greenhouse gases with the trends predicted in previous IPCC reports. The increase of global fossil fuel carbon dioxide emissions in the past decade has averaged 0.6% per year, which is somewhat below the range of IPCC scenarios, and the same is true for atmospheric methane concentrations. It is not known whether these slowdowns in growth rate will persist.

How much of the expected climate change is the consequence of climate feedback processes (e.g., water vapor, clouds, snow packs)?

The contribution of feedbacks to the climate change depends upon "climate sensitivity," as described in the report. If a central estimate of climate sensitivity is used, about 40% of the predicted warming is due to the direct effects of greenhouse gases and aerosols. The other 60% is caused by feedbacks. Water vapor feedback (the additional greenhouse effect accruing from increasing concentrations of atmospheric water vapor as the atmosphere warms) is the most important feedback in the models. Unless the relative humidity in the tropical middle and upper troposphere drops, this effect is expected to increase the temperature response to increases in human induced greenhouse gas concentrations by a factor of 1.6. The ice-albedo feedback (the reduction in the fraction of incoming solar radiation reflected back to space as snow and ice cover recede) also is believed to be important. Together, these two feedbacks amplify the simulated climate response to the greenhouse gas forcing by a factor of 2.5. In addition, changes in cloud cover, in the relative amounts of high versus low clouds, and in the mean and vertical distribution of relative humidity could either enhance or reduce the amplitude of the warming. Much of the difference in predictions of global warming by various climate models is attributable to the fact that each model represents these processes in its own particular way. These uncertainties will remain until a more fundamental understanding of the processes that control atmospheric relative humidity and clouds is achieved.

What will be the consequences (e.g., extreme weather, health effects) of increases of various magnitude?

In the near term, agriculture and forestry are likely to benefit from carbon dioxide fertilization and an increased water efficiency of some plants at higher atmospheric CO_2 concentrations. The optimal climate for crops may change, requiring significant regional adaptations. Some models project an increased tendency toward drought over semi-arid regions, such as the U.S. Great Plains. Hydrologic impacts could be significant over the western

United States, where much of the water supply is dependent on the amount of snow pack and the timing of the spring runoff. Increased rainfall rates could impact pollution run-off and flood control. With higher sea level, coastal regions could be subject to increased wind and flood damage even if tropical storms do not change in intensity. A significant warming also could have far reaching implications for ecosystems. The costs and risks involved are difficult to quantify at this point and are, in any case, beyond the scope of this brief report.

Health outcomes in response to climate change are the subject of intense debate. Climate is one of a number of factors influencing the incidence of infectious disease. Cold-related stress would decline in a warmer climate, while heat stress and smog induced respiratory illnesses in major urban areas would increase, if no adaptation occurred. Over much of the United States, adverse health outcomes would likely be mitigated by a strong public health system, relatively high levels of public awareness, and a high standard of living.

Global warming could well have serious adverse societal and ecological impacts by the end of this century, especially if globally-averaged temperature increases approach the upper end of the IPCC projections. Even in the more conservative scenarios, the models project temperatures and sea levels that continue to increase well beyond the end of this century, suggesting that assessments that examine only the next 100 years may well underestimate the magnitude of the eventual impacts.

Has science determined whether there is a "safe" level of concentration of greenhouse gases?

The question of whether there exists a "safe" level of concentration of greenhouse gases cannot be answered directly because it would require a value judgment of what constitutes an acceptable risk to human welfare and ecosystems in various parts of the world, as well as a more quantitative assessment of the risks and costs associated with the various impacts of global warming. In general, however, risk increases with increases in both the rate and the magnitude of climate change.

What are the substantive differences between the IPCC Reports and the Summaries?

The committee finds that the full IPCC Working Group I (WGI) report is an admirable summary of research activities in climate science, and the full report is adequately summarized in the *Technical Summary.* The full WGI report and its *Technical Summary* are not specifically directed at policy. The *Summary for Policymakers* reflects less emphasis on communicating the basis for uncertainty and a stronger emphasis on areas of major concern associated with human-induced climate change. This change in emphasis appears to be the result of a summary process in which scientists work with policymakers on the document. Written responses from U.S. coordinating and lead scientific authors to the committee indicate, however, that (a) no changes were made without the consent of the convening lead authors (this group represents a fraction of the lead and contributing authors) and (b) most changes that did occur lacked significant impact.

It is critical that the IPCC process remain truly representative of the scientific community. The committee's concerns focus primarily on whether the process is likely to become less representative in the future because of the growing voluntary time commitment required to participate as a lead or coordinating author and the potential that the scientific process will be viewed as being too heavily influenced by governments which have specific postures with regard to treaties, emission controls, and other policy instruments. The United States should promote actions that improve the IPCC process while also ensuring that its strengths are maintained.

What are the specific areas of science that need to be studied further, in order of priority, to advance our understanding of climate change?

Making progress in reducing the large uncertainties in projections of future climate will require addressing a number of fundamental scientific questions relating to the buildup of greenhouses gases in the atmosphere and the behavior of the climate system. Issues that need to be addressed include (a) the future usage of fossil fuels, (b) the future emissions of methane, (c) the fraction of the future fossil-fuel carbon that will remain in the atmosphere and provide radiative forcing versus exchange with the oceans or net exchange with the land biosphere, (d) the feedbacks in the climate system that determine both the magnitude of the change and the rate of energy uptake by the oceans, which together determine the magnitude and time history of the temperature increases for a given radiative forcing, (e) details of the regional and local climate change consequent to an overall level of global climate change, (f) the nature and causes of the natural variability of climate and its interactions with forced changes, and (g) the direct and indirect effects of the changing distributions of aerosols. Maintaining a vigorous, ongoing program of basic research, funded and managed independently of the climate assessment activity, will be crucial for narrowing these uncertainties.

In addition, the research enterprise dealing with environmental change and the interactions of human society with the environment must be enhanced. This includes support of (a) interdisciplinary research that couples physical, chemical, biological, and human systems, (b) an improved capability of integrating scientific knowledge, including its uncertainty, into effective decision support systems, and (c) an ability to conduct research at the regional or sectoral level that promotes analysis of the response of human and natural systems to multiple stresses.

An effective strategy for advancing the understanding of climate change also will require (1) a global observing system in support of long-term climate monitoring and prediction, (2) concentration on large-scale modeling through increased, dedicated supercomputing and human resources, and (3) efforts to ensure that climate research is supported and managed to ensure innovation, effectiveness, and efficiency.

APPENDIX D: SPEECH BY PRESIDENT GEORGE W. BUSH INTRODUCING CLEAR SKIES AND GLOBAL CLIMATE CHANGE INITIATIVES, FEBRUARY 14, 2002

On February 14, 2002, President George W. Bush introduced the administration's new Clear Skies and Global Climate Change Initiatives during a speech at the National Oceanic and Atmospheric Administration in Silver Spring, Maryland. Under pressure to announce his own climate policy following the withdrawal from the Kyoto process in March 2001, the president outlined a plan that emphasized sustained economic growth as the solution to global climate change. Reaffirming the U.S. commitment to the United Nations Framework Convention on Climate Change, the initiative included voluntary efforts that would reduce greenhouse gas intensity of the U.S. economy by 18 percent over ten years. ("Intensity" is the level of emissions normalized for the size of the economy—that is, the ratio of total U.S. emissions to GDP.) In addition, the plan promoted investment in science and technology, as well as investment in new clean technologies for developing countries. The following excerpt includes only the comments related to climate change; the full text is available online at: http://www.whitehouse.gov/news/releases/2002/02/20020214-5.html

February 14, 2002, 2:05 P.M. EST
THE PRESIDENT: Thank you very much for that warm welcome. It's an honor to join you all today to talk about our environment and about the prospect of dramatic progress to improve it.

Today, I'm announcing a new environmental approach that will clean our skies, bring greater health to our citizens and encourage environmentally responsible development in America and around the world.

[150]

Particularly, it's an honor to address this topic at NOAA, whose research is providing us with the answers to critical questions about our environment. And so I want to thank Connie for his hospitality and I want to thank you for yours, as well. Connie said he felt kind of like Sasha Cohen—I thought for a minute he was going to ask me to talk to his mother on his cell phone. (Laughter.)

I also want to tell you one of my favorite moments was to go down to Crawford and turn on my NOAA radio to get the weather. (Applause.) I don't know whether my guy is a computer or a person. (Laughter.) But the forecast is always accurate, and I appreciate that. I also want to thank you for your hard work, on behalf of the American people.

I appreciate my friend, Don Evans's leadership. I've known him for a long time. You're working for a good fellow, if you're working at the Commerce Department, or at NOAA. And I want to thank Spence Abraham and Christie Todd Whitman for their service to the country, as well. I've assembled a fabulous Cabinet, people who love their country and work hard. And these are three of some of the finest Cabinet officials I've got. (Applause.)

I want to thank Jim Connaughton, who is the Chairman of the Council on Environmental Quality. He's done a fabulous job of putting this policy together, a policy that I'm about to explain. But before I do, I also want to thank some members of Congress who have worked with us on this initiative. I want to thank Bob Smith and George Voinovich, two United States senators, for their leadership in pursuing multi-pollutant legislation; as well as Congressmen Billy Tauzin and Joe Barton. And I want to thank Senator Chuck Hagel and Larry Craig for their work on climate issues. These members of Congress have had an impact on the policies I am just about to announce.

America and the world share this common goal: we must foster economic growth in ways that protect our environment. We must encourage growth that will provide a better life for citizens, while protecting the land, the water, and the air that sustain life.

In pursuit of this goal, my government has set two priorities: we must clean our air, and we must address the issue of global climate change. We must also act in a serious and responsible way, given the scientific uncertainties. While these uncertainties remain, we can begin now to address the human factors that contribute to climate change. Wise action now is an insurance policy against future risks.

I have been working with my Cabinet to meet these challenges with forward and creative thinking. I said, if need be, let's challenge the status quo. But let's always remember, let's do what is in the interest of the American people.

Today, I'm confident that the environmental path that I announce will benefit the entire world. This new approach is based on this common-sense idea: that economic growth is key to environmental progress, because it is growth that provides the resources for investment in clean technologies.

This new approach will harness the power of markets, the creativity of entrepreneurs, and draw upon the best scientific research. And it will make possible a new partnership with the developing world to meet our common environmental and economic goals.

We will apply this approach first to the challenge of cleaning the air that Americans breathe. Today, I call for new Clean Skies legislation that sets tough new standards to dramatically reduce the three most significant forms of pollution from power plants, sulfur dioxide, nitrogen oxides and mercury. ...

[*The president discusses the Clean Skies Initiative, which will reduce sulfur dioxide emissions by 73 percent, nitrogen oxide emissions by 67 percent, and mercury emissions by 69 percent, all over two measured phases, the first ending in 2010 and the second in 2018.*]

Now, global climate change presents a different set of challenges and requires a different strategy. The science is more complex, the answers are less certain, and the technology is less developed. So we need a flexible approach that can adjust to new information and new technology.

I reaffirm America's commitment to the United Nations Framework Convention and its central goal, to stabilize atmospheric greenhouse gas concentrations at a level that will prevent dangerous human interference with the climate. Our immediate goal is to reduce America's greenhouse gas emissions relative to the size of our economy.

My administration is committed to cutting our nation's greenhouse gas intensity—how much we emit per unit of economic activity—by 18 percent over the next 10 years. This will set America on a path to slow the growth of our greenhouse gas emissions and, as science justifies, to stop and then reverse the growth of emissions.

This is the common-sense way to measure progress. Our nation must have economic growth—growth to create opportunity; growth to create a higher quality of life for our citizens. Growth is also what pays for investments in clean technologies, increased conservation, and energy efficiency. Meeting our commitment to reduce our greenhouse gas intensity by 18 percent by the year 2012 will prevent over 500 million metric tons of greenhouse gases from going into the atmosphere over the course of the decade. And that is the equivalent of taking 70 million cars off the road.

To achieve this goal, our nation must move forward on many fronts, looking at every sector of our economy. We will challenge American businesses to further reduce emissions. Already, agreements with the semiconductor and aluminum industries and others have dramatically cut emissions of some of the most potent greenhouse gases. We will build on these successes with new agreements and greater reductions.

Our government will also move forward immediately to create world-class standards for measuring and registering emission reductions. And we will give transferable credits to companies that can show real emission reductions.

We will promote renewable energy production and clean coal technology, as well as nuclear power, which produces no greenhouse gas emissions. And we will work to safely improve fuel economy for our cars and our trucks.

Overall, my budget devotes $4.5 billion to addressing climate change—more than any other nation's commitment in the entire world. This is an increase of more than $700 million over last year's budget. Our nation will continue to lead the world in basic climate and science research to address gaps in our knowledge that are important to decision makers.

When we make decisions, we want to make sure we do so on sound science; not what sounds good, but what is real. And the United States leads the world in providing that kind of research. We'll devote $588 million toward the research and development of energy conservation technologies. We must and we will conserve more in the United States. And we will spend $408 million toward research and development on renewables, on renewable energy.

This funding includes $150 million for an initiative that Spence Abraham laid out the other day, $150 million for the FreedomCar Initiative, which will advance the prospect of breakthrough zero-emission fuel cell technologies.

My comprehensive energy plan, the first energy plan that any administration has put out in a long period of time, provides $4.6 billion over the next five years in clean energy tax incentives to encourage purchases of hybrid and fuel cell vehicles, to promote residential solar energy, and to reward investments in wind, solar and biomass energy production. And we will look for ways to increase the amount of carbon stored by America's farms and forests through a strong conservation title in the farm bill. I have asked Secretary [Ann] Veneman to recommend new targeted incentives for landowners to increase carbon storage.

By doing all these things, by giving companies incentives to cut emissions, by diversifying our energy supply to include cleaner fuels, by increasing conservation, by increasing research and development and tax incentives for energy efficiency and clean technologies, and by increasing carbon storage, I am absolutely confident that America will reach the goal that I have set.

If, however, by 2012, our progress is not sufficient and sound science justifies further action, the United States will respond with additional measures that may include broad-based market programs as well as additional incentives and voluntary measures designed to accelerate technology development and deployment.

Addressing global climate change will require a sustained effort over many generations. My approach recognizes that economic growth is the solution, not the problem. Because a nation that grows its economy is a nation that can afford investments and new technologies.

The approach taken under the Kyoto protocol would have required the United States to make deep and immediate cuts in our economy to meet an arbitrary target. It would have cost our economy up to $400 billion and we would have lost 4.9 million jobs.

As President of the United States, charged with safeguarding the welfare of the American people and American workers, I will not commit our nation to an unsound international treaty that will throw millions of our citizens out of work. Yet, we recognize our international responsibilities. So in addition to acting here at home, the United States will actively help developing nations grow along a more efficient, more environmentally responsible path.

The hope of growth and opportunity and prosperity is universal. It's the dream and right of every society on our globe. The United States wants to foster economic growth in the developing world, including the world's poorest nations. We want to help them realize their potential, and bring the benefits of growth to their peoples, including better health, and better schools and a cleaner environment.

It would be unfair—indeed, counterproductive—to condemn developing nations to slow growth or no growth by insisting that they take on impractical and unrealistic greenhouse gas targets. Yet, developing nations such as China and India already account for a majority of the world's greenhouse gas emissions, and it would be irresponsible to absolve them from shouldering some of the shared obligations.

The greenhouse gas intensity approach I put forward today gives developing countries a yardstick for progress on climate change that recognizes their right to economic development. I look forward to discussing this new approach next week, when I go to China and Japan and South Korea. The United States will not interfere with the plans of any nation that chooses to ratify the Kyoto protocol. But I will intend to work with nations, especially the poor and developing nations, to show the world that there is a better approach, that we can build our future prosperity along a cleaner and better path.

My budget includes over $220 million for the U.S. Agency for International Development and a global environmental facility to help developing countries better measure, reduce emissions, and to help them invest in clean and renewable energy technologies. Many of these technologies, which we take for granted in our own country, are not being used in the developing world. We can help ensure that the benefits of these technologies are more broadly shared. Such efforts have helped bring solar energy to Bangladesh, hydroelectric energy to the Philippines, geothermal electricity to Kenya. These projects are bringing jobs and environmental benefits to these nations, and we will build on these successes.

The new budget also provides $40 million under the Tropical Forest Conservation Act to help countries redirect debt payments towards protecting tropical forests, forests that store millions of tons of carbon. And I've also ordered the Secretary of State to develop a new initiative to help developing countries stop illegal logging, a practice that destroys biodiversity and releases millions of tons of greenhouse gases into the atmosphere.

And, finally, my government is following through on our commitment to provide $25 million for climate observation systems in developing countries that will help scientists understand the dynamics of climate change.

To clean the air, and to address climate change, we need to recognize that economic growth and environmental protection go hand in hand. Affluent societies are the ones that demand, and can therefore afford, the most environmental protection. Prosperity is what allows us to commit more and more resources to environmental protection. And in the coming decades, the world needs to develop and deploy billions of dollars of technologies that generate energy in cleaner ways. And we need strong economic growth to make that possible.

Americans are among the most creative people in our history. We have used radio waves to peer into the deepest reaches of space. We cracked life's genetic code. We have made our air and land and water significantly cleaner, even as we have built the world's strongest economy.

When I see what Americans have done, I know what we can do. We can tap the power of economic growth to further protect our environment for generations that follow. And that's what we're going to do.

Thank you. (Applause.)

APPENDIX E: FURTHER READING

The literature on the causes, consequences, and policy responses concerning climate change is vast. The following is a brief introduction, with emphasis on sources that are available on the web and sources that focus on issues relevant for U.S. policy. To offer a manageable drink from the fountain rather than a firehose of completeness, much excellent material has been omitted.

ON THE CAUSES AND CONSEQUENCES OF CLIMATE CHANGE:

For the most comprehensive international reports on the causes and possible consequences of climate change, see the results of the Intergovernmental Panel on Climate Change at http://www.ipcc.ch

These reports have framed much of the debate; however, the U.S. government has also periodically asked the National Academy of Sciences to investigate particular issues. For several of their most important reports, see:

- "Reconciling Observations of Global Temperature Change" (2000): http://books.nap.edu/books/0309068916/html/
- "Climate Change Science: An Analysis of Some Key Questions" (2001): http://books.nap.edu/books/0309075742/html/
- "Abrupt Climate Change: Inevitable Surprises" (2002): http://books.nap.edu/openbook/0309074347/html/
- "Effectiveness and Impact of Corporate Average Fuel Economy (CAFE) Standards" (2002): http://books.nap.edu/books/0309076013/html/
- "The Hydrogen Economy: Opportunities, Costs, Barriers, and R&D Needs" (2004): http://books.nap.edu/books/0309091632/html/

For more on the impacts of climate change in the United States, see the National Assessment; the main findings are reprinted in Appendix B; complete text at http://www.usgcrp.gov/usgcrp/nacc/default.htm

For one of several research groups engaged in the integrated study of the scientific, economic, and policy aspects of climate change, see:
- http://web.mit.edu/globalchange/www

For more eclectic and highly opinionated accounts, here are two particularly active and irreverent sources:
- Stephen H. Schneider, "Climate Change": http://stephen schneider.stanford.edu/
- Science and Environmental Policy Project: http://www.sepp.org/

For an excellent history of the science, see:
- Spencer Weart, *The Discovery of Global Warming* (Cambridge: Harvard University Press, 2003)

ON THE ECONOMIC COSTS OF CONTROLLING EMISSIONS:

When Kyoto was taking shape there were many efforts to model the economic consequences. "The Costs of the Kyoto Protocol: A Multi-Model Evaluation," a far-ranging and systematic intercomparison of model results in Stanford University's Energy Modeling Forum (EMF), provides a good introduction to the results: http://www.iaee.org/en/publications/kyoto.aspx

The EMF also contributed heavily to the IPCC reports (cited above), and chapters in the report from IPCC Working Group #3 provide overviews of the issues and introduce in detail some of the controversies in economic modeling.

A key issue in assessing possible costs of control is the future structure of the world and regional energy systems. Here are two reports on that:
- On the world's energy systems generally, with assessments of key regions, see the International Energy Agency *World Energy Outlook* (2002) and *World Energy Investment Outlook* (2003): http://www.worldenergyoutlook.org/pubs/index.asp
- On emissions of greenhouse gases by the United States, see the EPA U.S. Emissions Inventory: http://yosemite.epa.gov/oar/ globalwarming.nsf/content/ResourceCenterPublications GHGEmissionsUSEmissionsInventory2004.html

- On future emissions, see the IPCC Special Report on Emission Scenarios (SRES): http://www.grida.no/climate/ipcc/emission/

Expectations about the prices and acceptability of major fuels will have a large impact on the cost of controlling carbon. For more, see the following:

- On natural gas and the current price spikes in the United States, see the National Petroleum Council report: http://www.npc.org/
- On nuclear power, which offers zero-carbon electricity but raises many questions about public acceptability, see: http://web.mit.edu/nuclearpower/
- On the role of LNG in natural gas markets, see James T. Jensen, "The LNG Revolution": http://www.energyseer.com/iaeepapr.pdf
- On the geopolitical consequences of a shift to a global gas market, see the Baker-Stanford study "The Geopolitics of Natural Gas": http://pesd.stanford.edu/gas
- On coal, which accounts for 51 percent of U.S. electric power production but is high in carbon, see the Energy Information Administration Annual Coal Report (2002): http://www.eia.doe.gov/cneaf/coal/page/acr/acr_sum.html
- On the quantities of energy scenarios for stabilizing the atmosphere, see Hoffert et al., "Energy Implications of Future Stabilization of Atmospheric CO_2 Content," Nature 395 (1998): 881-884: http://eed.llnl.gov/cccm/pdf/Hoffert_et_al_Nature.pdf
- On the costs of stabilizing CO_2 emissions, see T. Wigley, R. Richels, and J. Edmonds: "Economics and Environmental Choices in the Stabilization of Atmospheric CO_2 Concentrations," Nature, 379 (1996): 240-243

For more information on emerging emissions trading systems, see:

- The European Union's emissions trading scheme: http://europa.eu.int/comm/environment/climat/emission.htm
- The Chicago Climate Exchange: http://chicagoclimate exchange.com

ON INNOVATION AND THE DESIGN OF TECHNOLOGY POLICIES:
Most of the relevant literature on technology policy is not written with the climate change problem in mind, as the question of whether and how the government can successfully intervene in the process of innovation is a generic one. For some windows into that literature, see:
- Richard R. Nelson, *National Innovation Systems: A Comparative Analysis* (Oxford: Oxford University Press, 1991)
- Linda R. Cohen and Roger G. Noll, *The Technology Pork Barrel* (Washington, DC: Brookings Institution Press, 1991)
- UNESCO *World Science Report* (1998): http://www.unesco.org/science/publication/eng_pub/wsren.htm
- Benn Steil, David G. Victor, and Richard R. Nelson, eds., *Technology Innovation and Economic Performance* (Princeton: Princeton University Press, 2002)

For such work focused specifically on energy, see:
- President's Committee of Advisors on Science and Technology (PCAST), Panel on Energy Research and Development (1997): http://neri.ne.doe.gov/docs/pcast/cover.pdf
- James J. Dooley (Pacific Northwest National Laboratory), "Energy Research and Development: Global Trends in Policy and Investment" (1999): http://energytrends.pnl.gov/
- Electric Power Research Institute, "About Strategic Science and Technology" (2004): http://www.epri.com/programDesc.asp?program=255855

ON INTERNATIONAL COOPERATION:
Key international agreements (the United Nations Framework Convention on Climate Change and the Kyoto Protocol), information on activities under those agreements, such as the Clean Development Mechanism (CDM), and links to government-reported data on emissions and policies can be found at http://unfccc.int

On the Prototype Carbon Fund, which aims to jump-start the CDM, see: http://www.prototypecarbonfund.org

ON THE DESIGN OF INTERNATIONAL ARCHITECTURES:

There is a large and growing literature on international "architectures" or "regimes" to address climate change. Much of it is based on analogies with other areas of international cooperation on environmental and economic problems as well as analogies with policy instruments that have been used to address national environmental problems, such as the sulfur dioxide emission trading program used in the United States. For some windows into that huge literature, see:

- Thomas C. Schelling, "Costs and Benefits of Greenhouse Gas Reduction," American Enterprise Institute Studies on Global Environmental Policy (Washington, DC: AEI Press, 1998)
- M. Granger Morgan, "Climate Change: Managing Carbon from the Bottom Up," *Science* 289 (2000): 2285
- David G. Victor, *The Collapse of the Kyoto Protocol and the Struggle to Slow Global Warming* (Princeton: Princeton University Press, 2001)
- Scott Barrett, *Environment and Statecraft: The Strategy of Environmental Treaty-Making* (Oxford: Oxford University Press, 2003)
- Joseph E. Aldy, Scott Barrett, and Robert N. Stavins, "Thirteen Plus One: A Comparison of Global Climate Policy Architectures," Faculty Research Working Paper Series, John F. Kennedy School of Government, Harvard University (2003): http://www.ksg.harvard.edu/cbg/eephu/Thirteen_plus_one.pdf
- Richard B. Stewart and Jonathan B. Wiener, *Reconstructing Climate Policy: Beyond Kyoto* (Washington, DC: AEI Press, 2003)
- Pew Center on Global Climate Change, "Beyond Kyoto: Advancing the International Effort Against Climate Change" (2003): http://www.pewclimate.org/global-warming-in-depth/all_reports/beyond_kyoto/index.cfm

ON PUBLIC ATTITUDES:

There have been many polls on climate change policy, and poll data require careful interpretation. The best introduction to the results and sensitivity to issues such as the framing of questions is the Program on International Policy Attitudes: http://www.pipa.org/

In addition, researchers have struggled with the question of how to frame information about complex and uncertain scientific issues so that it is comprehensible and conveyed accurately. For the fullest project in this spirit, see the Center for Integrated Study of the Human Dimensions of Global Change: http://hdgc.epp.cmu.edu/

ON POLITICAL ACTIVISM:

There are many organizations large and small with a view on what is happening with the climate and how policymakers in the United States (and other countries) should respond. Here is a sampling of the field:

- BP on climate: http://www.bp.com/genericsection.do?cate goryId=931&contentId=2016995
- California Climate Action Registry: http://www.climateregistry.org
- Center for Environmental Leadership in Business: http://www.celb.org
- Climate Action Network: http://www.climatenetwork.org/
- Competitive Enterprise Institute: http://www.cei.org
- Conservation International: http://conservation.org
- Environmental Defense: http://www.edf.org/system/tem plates/page/focus.cfm?focus=3
- ExxonMobil on climate: www2.exxonmobil.com/corporate/ citizenship/corp_citizenship_enviro_overview.asp
- Heritage Foundation: http://www.heritage.org/research/ener gyandenvironment/issues2004.cfm
- National Environmental Trust: http://www.net.org/
- National Resources Defense Council: http://www.nrdc.org
- Pew Center on Global Climate Change, which offers the most elaborate of all these websites and includes extensive issue briefs: http://www.pewclimate.org
- Union of Concerned Scientists: http://www.ucsusa.org/
- World Wildlife Fund: http://www.worldwildlife.org/cli mate/climate.cfm

ON U.S. GOVERNMENT POLICIES AND APPROACHES AND
ENVIRONMENTAL ISSUES IN THE 2004 PRESIDENTIAL CAMPAIGN:

President Bush has spoken about climate change issues several times: http://www.whitehouse.gov/infocus/environment/

In the Bush administration, the Council on Environmental Quality has played a central role in formulating policy on climate change: http://www.whitehouse.gov/ceq/

For the foreign policy aspects, see the Department of State Global Issues office: http://usinfo.state.gov/gi/global_issues/climate_change.html

For the 2003 Climate Stewardship Act (Senate Resolution 139) sponsored by Senators John McCain and Joseph Lieberman, see http://www.theorator.com/bills108/s139.html and for an analysis of the resolution, see http://www.eia.doe.gov/oiaf/servicerpt/ml/pdf/summary.pdf

For more on the organization of U.S. investment in climate science, see:

- The United States Global Change Research Program (http://www.usgcrp.gov/) and the United States Climate Change Science Program (http://www.climatescience.gov/USGCRP)
- The National Academy of Sciences review of the USCCSP (2004): http://www4.nationalacademies.org/news.nsf/isbn/0309088658?OpenDocument
- The National Oceanic and Atmospheric Administration: http://www.noaa.gov/climate.html
- Lawrence Berkeley National Laboratory: http://www esd.lbl.gov/CLIMATE/index.html
- The Environmental Protection Agency: http://yosemite.epa.gov/oar/globalwarming.nsf/content/index.html

For more on the U.S. investment in technology, see:

- United States Climate Change Technology Program: http://www.climatetechnology.gov/about/
- FreedomCAR and Vehicle Technologies Program: http://avt.inel.gov/
- FutureGen Initiative: http://www.fossil.energy.gov/programs/powersystems/futuregen/

CPI ADVISORY COMMITTEE

TONY BRENTON
Embassy of the United Kingdom of Great Britain and Northern Ireland

WALTER F. BUCHHOLTZ
ExxonMobil Corporation

JACQUES DUBOIS
Swiss Re America Corporation

JEFFREY A. FRANKEL
Harvard University

DAVID HAWKINS
Natural Resources Defense Council

DALE E. HEYDLAUFF
American Electric Power Services

CONNIE HOLMES
National Mining Association

JAMES M. LINDSAY
Council on Foreign Relations

M. GRANGER MORGAN
Carnegie Mellon University

CHRIS MOTTERSHEAD
BP

PAUL PORTNEY
Resources for the Future

DAN REICHER
New Energy Capital

STEPHEN H. SCHNEIDER
Stanford University

DIANE WITTENBERG
California Climate Action Registry

ABOUT THE AUTHOR

David G. Victor is Director of the Program on Energy and Sustainable Development at Stanford University and adjunct senior fellow at the Council on Foreign Relations in New York. The program at Stanford, launched in September 2001, focuses on electricity and gas markets worldwide. Dr. Victor teaches international environmental politics in the Political Science Department at Stanford University and energy law at Stanford Law School.

Previously, Dr. Victor directed the Science and Technology program at the Council on Foreign Relations, where he studied the sources of technological innovation and the impact of innovation on economic growth. His research also examined global forest policy, global warming, and genetic engineering of food crops. His Ph.D. is from the Massachusetts Institute of Technology (Political Science and International Relations), his B.A. from Harvard University (History and Science).

His publications include *The Collapse of the Kyoto Protocol and the Struggle to Slow Global Warming* (Princeton University Press, 2001), *Technological Innovation and Economic Performance* (Princeton University Press, 2002, co-edited with Benn Steil and Richard Nelson), and an edited book of case studies on the implementation of international environmental agreements (MIT Press, 1998). He is author of numerous essays and articles in scholarly journals and magazines and newspapers, including *Climatic Change, The Financial Times, Foreign Affairs, International Journal of Hydrogen Energy, Nature, The New York Times, Scientific American,* and *The Washington Post.*